# ROUTLEDGE LIBRARY EDITIONS: WW2

Volume 38

# VICTORY OR VESTED INTEREST?

# VICTORY OR VESTED INTEREST?

G.D.H. COLE, HAROLD LASKI, GEORGE ORWELL, MARY SUTHERLAND AND FRANCIS WILLIAMS

LONDON AND NEW YORK

First published in 1942 by George Routledge & Sons, Ltd.

This edition first published in 2022
by Routledge
2 Park Square, Milton Park, Abingdon, Oxon OX14 4RN

and by Routledge
605 Third Avenue, New York, NY 10158

*Routledge is an imprint of the Taylor & Francis Group, an informa business*

© 1942 George Routledge & Sons, Ltd.

All rights reserved. No part of this book may be reprinted or reproduced or utilised in any form or by any electronic, mechanical, or other means, now known or hereafter invented, including photocopying and recording, or in any information storage or retrieval system, without permission in writing from the publishers.

*Trademark notice*: Product or corporate names may be trademarks or registered trademarks, and are used only for identification and explanation without intent to infringe.

*British Library Cataloguing in Publication Data*
A catalogue record for this book is available from the British Library

ISBN: 978-1-03-201217-9 (Set)
ISBN: 978-1-00-319367-8 (Set) (ebk)
ISBN: 978-1-03-203661-8 (Volume 38) (hbk)
ISBN: 978-1-03-203665-6 (Volume 38) (pbk)
ISBN: 978-1-00-318839-1 (Volume 38) (ebk)

DOI: 10.4324/9781003188391

**Publisher's Note**
The publisher has gone to great lengths to ensure the quality of this reprint but points out that some imperfections in the original copies may be apparent.

**Disclaimer**
The publisher has made every effort to trace copyright holders and would welcome correspondence from those they have been unable to trace.

# VICTORY
## OR VESTED INTEREST
## ?

*by* G. D. H. COLE, HAROLD LASKI
GEORGE ORWELL, MARY SUTHERLAND
FRANCIS WILLIAMS

LONDON
GEORGE ROUTLEDGE & SONS, LTD.
BROADWAY HOUSE : 68–74 CARTER LANE, E.C.

*First published 1942*

NOTE
THIS BOOK IS PRODUCED IN COMPLETE CONFORMITY WITH THE AUTHORIZED ECONOMY STANDARDS

Printed in Great Britain by Butler & Tanner Ltd., Frome and London

# CONTENTS

| | | PAGE |
|---|---|---|
| NOTE . . . . . . . . | | vii |
|    *by* John Parker | | |
| 1 PRIVATE MONOPOLY OR PUBLIC SERVICE . . | | 1 |
|    *by* G. D. H. Cole | | |
| 2 EQUALITY OF SACRIFICE . . . . . | | 22 |
|    *by* Francis Williams | | |
| 3 DEMOCRACY IN WAR TIME . . . . . | | 38 |
|    *by* Harold J. Laski | | |
| 4 WOMEN AND THE WAR . . . . . | | 57 |
|    *by* Mary Sutherland | | |
| 5 CULTURE AND DEMOCRACY . . . . . | | 77 |
|    *by* George Orwell | | |

## NOTE

OWING to the difficulty of arranging publication rights, it is regretted that Mr. Victor Gollancz's lecture has had to be omitted from this volume.

# NOTE

These essays are based on a series of lectures delivered under the auspices of the Fabian Society. They represent not the collective view of the Society, but those of the individual contributors. The Society's responsibility is limited to approving the contents as embodying facts and opinions worthy of consideration within the Labour Movement.

The aims of the Society are the furtherance of socialism and the education of the public on socialist lines. Membership is open to all who are prepared to accept the Constitution of the Labour Party, and people of all progressive points of view are invited to become associates.

The offices of the Society are at 11 Dartmouth Street, S.W.1.

JOHN PARKER, M.P.,
*General Secretary,*
*Fabian Society.*

# VICTORY OR VESTED INTEREST?

## 1. PRIVATE MONOPOLY OR PUBLIC SERVICE

*by* G. D. H. COLE

This is a war in which no available waste can be afforded, either of materials, or of machinery, or of men. It is often given the name of " total war ", to indicate that it requires the use of all our resources, either directly in waging it or in producing necessary supplies to keep the people in condition to carry it through to the end. It is a struggle in which we cannot afford to hold back anything that can be of help in the war effort, because we are face to face with an immensely strong and determined enemy, who is already waging total war, and is intent not simply on defeating us in arms but on destroying our entire civilisation and on condemning those of us whom he suffers to survive at all to a future of penury and enslavement. Against such an enemy we too must wage " total war " ; but we are sorely reluctant to follow his example, because we are a thoroughly untotalitarian people, and accustomed to dislike regimentation more than we like order, and to value our personal freedom more highly than the claims of citizenship—at any rate until we are driven to understand that we cannot have the one except by defending the other.

But by this time, you say, we surely are roused, as a people, to defend our rights. Have we not put up, not merely with military conscription but with quite a large instalment of industrial conscription as well? Are not women, as well as men, being compelled to serve where they are needed? Is not Income Tax at ten shillings in the pound, with surtax over and above, for those who are fortunate enough to have to pay it? Is not Excess Profits Tax, at any rate nominally, fixed at one hundred per cent.? Are we not all rationed, so that we cannot even blow our noses without a coupon? Has not the Government power to do pretty well what it chooses with any of us, without compensation too? Are we not all slaves already, and our cherished liberties gone in the process of fighting for them?

Well, not quite. The Government, I agree, is armed with immense powers, and has actually used some of these powers in ways which involve a great curtailment of popular liberties. A large number of persons, soldiers and munition workers, men and women, are being compelled to do things which cause them serious loss of freedom and often great hardship. The vast majority of those upon whom these blows have fallen are bearing them without complaint, though naturally not without an occasional grumble. They are bearing them because they recognize the necessity for them, and understand that far worse calamities would fall upon them if the war were lost. They are even, in certain directions, crying out to be asked to make more sacrifices. Nothing in this war is more remarkable than the way in which the trade unions of skilled workers have actually taken the lead in pressing for the dilution of labour, at the cost of giving up their cherished customs and regulations. The trade unionists have from the very beginning cried out for more production as a means to victory, and have been ready to pay the price. The Minister who has been responsible for introducing the most galling restrictions on the personal freedom of the workers is a leading trade unionist; and his actions have by no means weakened his hold upon those whom he represents.

And yet . . . we are still a long way off waging total war. For though we have gone a long way towards conscripting labour for the national effort, we have advanced much less far towards the conscription of capital. We have, it is true, established a large measure of control over the employer. In the war trades, nearly all firms are working largely on government contracts and all firms depend on the government " controls " for their supplies of materials, fuel, and new capital equipment, as well as of labour. In a number of other trades, working for the civilian market or for export, there has been enforced " concentration ", which has totally closed down some firms for the duration of the war and enforced pooling in order to achieve economies in the use of materials, machines, factory space, and human hands. To a considerable extent the employer, as well as the workman, is under orders; and it is true nearly everywhere that the profit incentive, on which reliance used to be placed for securing efficient production, is nearly in abeyance, because almost every productive business that remains in operation can rely, without any difficulty, on making at least as much profit as it will be allowed to retain.

And yet . . . we are still a long way off waging total war. For, save in the rarest cases, the employer is still the employer, whether he is pulling his weight in the national interest or not. There is power, by Act of Parliament, to turn out the farmer who fails to farm his land efficiently; and a few farmers, mostly elderly men, have actually been turned out by the County Agricultural Committees. There is power to turn out inefficient factory managements, or boards of directors, in the war trades; but I believe those who have been turned out could be counted on the fingers of one hand. The prewar firms, with their boards of directors and their managing officials, good, bad or indifferent, are still where they were. Managers of the most vital establishments are still the servants of private firms or combines, and not of the State. The firm, not the State, appoints, pays, promotes or dismisses them : they remain responsible to the directors, representing the private owners of the invested capital, and not to the public.

In other words, we are fighting this war, in its economic aspect, under the institutions of private capitalism. The working of these institutions has, of course, been greatly affected by war-time control. But the institutions themselves remain in being : the State works through them, and does not attempt to supersede them. Nay, more : the State does not even give these private firms direct orders to produce this or that in the public interest. It enters into contracts with them—invites them to tender for producing so much of one thing and so much of another—strikes in each case a bargain for the use of the firm's services, on terms which usually involve the earning of a handsome profit on the transaction—a profit which, beyond a prescribed limit, is subsequently recovered by the Chancellor of the Exchequer by means of taxation.

This, when you come to think about it, is a very remarkable method of organizing war production. At first sight it would seem plain common sense, when the State is the sole customer, or at any rate by far the most important, for the war factories to be taken over, lock, stock and barrel, for the duration of the war, and for their owners to be paid merely such rates for the use of the premises as might seem just and expedient in the circumstances. It would seem that, if this were done, the State would have a much freer hand in organizing the factories to serve the nation's needs—to plan output, to dovetail the machine and labour capacities of neighbouring establishments, to get rid of inefficient managements and unwanted directors, to promote efficient men to positions of wider responsibility, to shift men or machines about from one factory to another, and in sum to disregard all considerations other than the overriding consideration of causing each factory to make the largest possible contribution to the total war effort.

Why, then, is this not done? Why, when we have conscripted men, have we made only a faint pretence of conscripting capital? Why does the capitalist firm survive as the unit of war production, though it is quite plainly, from the technical standpoint, not the right unit? Why retain all the *paperasserie* of making separate contracts and sub-contracts and sub-sub-contracts, often half a dozen deep, instead of cutting away all the dead wood, and organizing the war trades, simply and directly, as a branch of the public service?

There are two reasons; but let us take one of them first. When this war began, under the auspices of the unwilling Chamberlain Government, the cry was " business as usual " all along the line. Behind the policy of " appeasement " had been the fear that war, if it came, might undermine the structure of private capitalism; and this fear continued to rule the minds of our politicians all through that calamitous first year of anything but total war. The orders that went out to the departments were still to interfere as little as possible with the working of " private enterprise "; and, where considerable interference was unavoidable, as it was in the rationing of scarce materials and the control of their production, the orders were to leave the business people engaged in these lines of supply to do the controlling themselves, as agents of the State.

The consequence was the installation of those remarkable " controls " at the Ministry of Supply—and largely at other Ministries also—controls which appeared to be little else than the pre-war trusts and associations operating under another name. The staffs of the great combines moved bodily into the Government offices, and became the State's agents, wielding a public power which replaced or reinforced the power they had hitherto wielded as private bodies. The Ministry of Supply, in particular, was hardly in any ordinary sense a ministry at all ; the greater part of it consisted of almost independent controls of the kind I have described, operating with very little regard to the Minister nominally responsible for them. This applied especially to the parts of the Ministry which dealt with materials and semi-manufactures. It was less true of the sections which had to deal with the placing of contracts for finished arms and other war goods. But much the same spirit permeated the entire Ministry. In the case of materials power was exercised by and through the great monopolistic combines : in the case of finished goods it was exercised more through individual firms. But there too the great firm which was in effect a combine in itself became the Ministry's agent for dealing with a host of sub-contractors with most of whom the Government had no direct relations.

The consequence was an almost unbelievable haphazardness in the placing of war orders. There was no real plan of production : everything was improvised and, when one thing after another went wrong, a patch was put hastily on the weak spot, without any attempt to remove the cause which had led to the mishaps. It is true that some of these improvisations were remarkable. The great increase of war output which followed the terrible loss of war equipment in France in the spring of 1940 was a wonderful effort. But it had all the characteristics of a " soldiers' battle ", fought by workers and

managers in the factories almost without generalship—
though one " general ", Lord Beaverbrook, did improve
the occasion to the extent of making his mark as a talented
guerrilla chieftain. The workers in the factories, and
many of the managers, wrought wonders during the
ensuing months ; and their energy saved this country
from irreparable disaster. But even that effort was an
improvisation, and did not rest on any plan. For a few
months men wore themselves out in a heroic struggle for
higher production ; but even at the height of the struggle,
investigation showed that many vital machine tools were
standing idle for a large part of every week, and that
while some men were working like blacks others were
standing idle because necessary materials or subcon-
tracted components had failed to arrive to time, or
because designs had been suddenly changed or factories
were short of indispensable skilled workers, while in the
factory next door the needed workers were standing idle
or engaged on unnecessary peace-time work. There was
muddle everywhere ; and the main source of the muddle,
I am sure, was that we were attempting to carry on war
production through and on the advice of the very capitalist
agencies which had already failed us lamentably in the
days of peace.

For do not forget that throughout the inter-war period
the first thought of nearly all the great capitalist combines
had been to prevent, and not to stimulate, production.
The aim of almost every combine had been, not merely
to prevent fresh competitors from entering the trade, but
to drive out of it as many as possible of those who were
in it already. It had been discovered that the safest—
many said the only—way of maintaining profits was to
keep goods scarce and prices high. In the sacred name of
" rationalization ", works regarded as " redundant " had
been bought up and razed to the ground, or otherwise

effectually put out of business. Shipbuilders' Security, the Iron and Steel Federation, the cement combine, and a host of others had been highly successful at this monopolist game; and the business quality highest in estimation had come to be that of making one blade of grass grow where two or three could have been grown without any technical difficulty. Was it likely that financial directors trained in this restrictive school would be good at organizing production when the sky became the limit? They were not good at it: they were very bad. But they were the men whom Chamberlain had designated to lead the economic effort of war; and even after the fall of France there were plenty of pundits who told us of the terrible danger of swopping horses in mid-stream.

Things have improved since then: for a certain degree of planning and organization has been forced upon the country by imperative needs. But much of the old confusion remains, and is bound to remain as long as we attempt to organize production on the basis of treating each capitalist firm as a sacrosanct entity, instead of using the entire equipment and labour supply in each area as a single pool, and making our arrangements on a technical instead of a financial basis.

Let no one suppose that what I have been saying is meant as abuse of the technical and managerial staffs of industry. There are among them good, bad and indifferent, probably in much the same proportions as in other callings. What I am complaining of is not that they do their work badly, even though some of them do: it is that they cannot be expected to do it well, under war conditions, when they are in effect having to serve two masters—the State, which needs the product of their organizing labours, and the financial directorates by which they are employed, and expect to go on being employed when the war is over. They cannot help being torn between two loyalties, and two sets of considerations—the desire to secure maximum output now, for war purposes, and the desire not to prejudice the profit-earning capacity of their firms after the war. They would be free of the divided mind, or at any rate freer of it, if for the war period the factories were taken over completely by the State, and if the State could move them freely from one establishment to another, giving the most successful the largest responsibilities, and putting the less efficient either out of the job or under the supervision of those managers who showed the greater drive and capacity for large-scale organization.

I have been speaking so far exclusively of one of the reasons why production is not better organized in this third year of the war. But I said at the outset that there were two reasons; and it is high time to turn to the other. I have been trying to show that, from one aspect, it would be plain common sense for the State to take over the big war factories and run them for the war period as really public concerns. But, apart from the reluctance to interfere with the vested interests of existing big business, there is a second reason why many people feel reluctant for this to be done. They do not want industry to be run by the Civil Service.

It is indeed painfully clear that civil service control is no guarantee of efficient management. Some of the big State factories which have been erected either during or shortly before the war are among the most notoriously inefficient producing agencies at the present time. Some have even been taken out of the hands of those who were managing them for the State, and have been put under the management of private firms; and for all I know to the contrary the change may have been a positive benefit. One can trust the State organization which the Ministry of Supply took over from the War Office even less than one can trust the more efficient private firms to administer competently the business of war production. It is exceedingly foolish for Socialists to speak, as they are sometimes inclined to do, as if State ownership were in itself a guarantee of efficiency. It is nothing of the sort. Efficiency depends on more than one factor. It requires, in connection with productive organization, at least four things. The first of these is a high quality of factory management on both the organizing and the technical side. The second is a clear and competent central direction, which will both give sensible and explicit orders to each factory, and ensure a right co-ordination in the arrival of supplies of materials, machinery, and in these days, of labour as well. The working out and application of a well-considered scheme of priorities is one aspect of this : a well-controlled department of design in each main branch of output is another ; and yet another is a skilled and unpedantic inspection department, which will allow factory managements and skilled workers reasonable freedom in the adaptation of designs to fit in with the realities of factory equipment and with the requirements of the assembly shop. The third condition is a contented and keen labour force, which cannot be secured unless there is competence in the organization responsible for allotting labour, and some rationality in the wage-payments made to workers for different degrees of skill, effort, and sacrifice—for example, in travelling long distances to and from work. The fourth condition is that there shall be no authority in a position to work against the aim of raising production to the highest possible point—no conflict in the managers' minds between conflicting loyalties, and no twisting of effort, under the impulse of the profit-motive, away from the fullest satisfaction of public needs.

State ownership and operation directly guarantee only the last of these four conditions. A mere change to public ownership will not turn an inefficient into an efficient manager, or improve the quality of design or inspection, or ensure a right system of priorities, or make the workers contented if they are not getting a square deal or if their labour is badly distributed and wrongly used. Nor is it in the least true that Civil Servants are better at running industry than the people who have been used to running it. Indeed, their training in a very different routine, which involves a great deal of splitting up of responsibility and a constant necessity of acting according to precedent in order to avoid trouble, renders them very unsuitable agents for carrying through the quick changes and wholesale readaptations which war requires. If we had to choose between having our war industries run with meticulous honesty by the methods of civil-service routine, and having them run by piratical business men intent on snatching the maximum profit for themselves, I think we should be driven to choose to be the victims of piracy rather than of stolidity, and to let the profiteers exploit us rather than lose the war before the Civil Servants could have time to devise a new set of precedents to fit the new needs.

But we do not have to make this choice. Nobody wants the Civil Service to run our industries—or at any rate nobody who matters. The only persons who can possibly manage industry, in peace or in war, are those who have been trained to manage it, and are in command of the requisite knowledge and skill. The question is not what class of persons is to manage our industries, but under what auspices and impulsions the running of them is to be done.

What I am contending is that our managers and technicians could make a much better job of managing and organizing our industries if they were doing it, not in a " dual capacity ", half for the State and half for the boards of directors which pay their salaries, but wholly for the public. I have no objection at all to high officials of big business occupying high positions in the war-time public service, provided that in becoming public servants they do really shed their capitalist connections. I should like to see all boards of directors of big companies simply given their *congé*, all shareholders accorded for the war period a fixed rate of compensation payable directly by the State, and all the managerial and technical staffs of the big private concerns simply taken over, and paid fixed salaries by the State. But something more than this is involved. I do not want to confiscate anybody's property without reasonable compensation; but I do want it to be understood that, when the State takes over the war factories, there is no assurance that it will ever hand them back to the same body of private owners. For, if such an assurance is given, no temporary taking over by the State will be able to prevent the managers from having divided minds, and thinking not only of the war effort, but also of what their directors and principal shareholders will say to them when they return to their service after the war, if in the meantime they have damaged the future profit-earning capacity of their factories in the interests of victory.

I believe, then, that what is needed is not mere temporary taking over, but nationalization outright—on a basis which will leave the future ownership and management of the big productive agencies to be settled after the war, in the light of the situation which then exists. I am not asking for a guarantee that public ownership or management *will* continue—for that would be at variance with the conditions of political coalition on which we are fighting the war. I am asking that the future be left open—which is, after all, the only condition that is really consistent with the political composition of the War Government.

What I want to secure by this is not more civil-service control of industry, but more unfettered control by the best managers and technicians who can be found. I should like to take the best man available, and give him the management not of one factory but of many—telling him to get on with the job of co-ordinating a whole group of complementary establishments into a single productive unit, quite irrespective of the previous ownerships. I should like machines and workers and contracts to be freely movable from one factory to another, without all the complications which arise at present out of the separate ownership of the various plants. I should like to turn the Regional Boards which now exist with very limited powers under the Production Executive into real executive and planning agencies, with the job of ensuring the fullest possible use of all the available resources of production within their areas. In effect, I want public ownership, not because I regard it as being, in itself, a guarantee of efficient working, but because I do not see how the measures needed for achieving efficiency can be taken except on a basis of public ownership.

Please observe that I am not asking for the nationalization of the smaller factories, except where it is necessary in order to round off a particular productive group. I believe that, given the public ownership of the big factories and a proper plan for their reorganization, the smaller firms will be able to work in much more efficiently than they can at present. I do not want to take over the little factories, because that would place too great a task upon those responsible for making the change, and also because the owners of the smaller factories are usually working managers as well as owners, and not primarily financial wizards. The smaller fry will have, of course, to conform to the requirements of the public plan ; but, if there is a plan, they can be made to work in with it without being actually taken over. There must be power to displace such men when they fail to pull their weight—or rather, this power, which exists already, must be actually used. If it is used, it will suffice. The factories which need taking over are those which belong to the big financiers, including the monopolists. In wartime we cannot afford to embark on nationalization for nationalization's sake, but only where the need for it is plainly apparent.

I have spoken of factories ; but of course the case holds good for other productive agencies as well. For ships, for example, and for railways, and for all forms of transport run by large concerns. It holds good for mines, and for wholesale agencies, including the great importers and the wholesale distributors of foodstuffs. The position is not, however, in any of these industries quite the same as in munition-making. For, whereas the munition makers are for the most part under the necessity of changing over to forms of production to which they are unused, and of radically adapting their factories to meet the needs of war, these other industries and services have, on the whole, to go on doing what they were doing before, though of course they too have to make many changes in method and organization as a result of war conditions. It remains, however, true of them, as well as of the munition-making industries, that a conflict may easily develop between what they ought to do for the furtherance of the war effort and what it suits them to do with a view to the resumption of normal profit-making in the future. Mine-owners can increase immediate output by concentrating entirely on the coal which is easiest to get ; but this will leave their pits more costly to operate when the emergency is over. Railway companies can postpone repairs and renewals to a greater or smaller extent. Importers and merchants can concentrate on the lines which can be purchased and distributed at the lowest real cost in transport and other charges, ignoring established connections which will be of value to them in post-war trading; or they can allow their decisions to be swayed to some extent by considerations which do nothing to bring victory nearer. Moreover, there is in all cases a strong inducement—the stronger because of E.P.T.—to get the Government to pay for capital improvements which will come in useful when normal conditions return—if they ever do.

There is, in effect, an unavoidable dualism in a system which involves the use of private, profit-seeking concerns as the agents of public policy. Nor is it the smallest disadvantage of this system that the persons whom it entrenches in public offices as the agents of the State are in general the representatives of large-scale business, and that these persons are bound, by virtue of their office, to acquire a very strong hold over the smaller businesses with which they have to deal. The last war left behind it a legacy of monopolistic organizations. In one case after another, the firms which had come together for the purpose of concerted dealings with the Government decided after the war to remain together, and became the combines and trade and industrial associations of to-day. This war has already carried that process a great deal further. It was not necessary, this time, for associations to be called into being for war purposes; for in the majority of instances they were there already. What has happened is that the associations have immensely strengthened their position, and have acquired very large powers over undertakings which had remained outside them, as well as over subsidiary businesses which depend on the big firms for supplies or orders for components.

I am not suggesting that this process of capitalist concentration is wholly bad. Indeed, something of the sort is plainly necessary for any kind of economic planning, in peace as well as in war. What is wrong about it is not the concentration of power, but the vesting of it in the hands of private combines animated by the motive of profit—the discordant blending of public and private monopolistic authority in the same hands.

We Socialists have, however, to face the fact that, if this dualism is to be avoided, we must find means of making industry responsive to the motive of public service without subjecting it to the inefficiencies of bureaucratic control. Private enterprise, however much it may involve monopoly, will continue to rule the roost as long as men think that bureaucracy is the only alternative. Already, recognizing this, the Labour Party and the trade unions have cast their plans for public ownership and administration of the vital industries into a form which is designed to avoid this danger. The Public Board or Corporation, and not the Civil Service Department, is the model on which plans for public enterprise are now almost universally based. This does not mean that Socialists are satisfied with the actual corporations which have been brought into existence—the Port of London Authority, the B.B.C., the Central Electricity Board, the London Passenger Transport Board, and some others. Each of these bodies suffers from its own defect. The P.L.A. is controlled too much by the wharfingers, and too little by the public. The B.B.C., in time of peace, is too little amenable to Parliamentary control. The C.E.B. has no effective hold over the great Power Companies. The L.P.T.B. is a most curious construction, with its extraordinary provision for appointing trustees and its legal obligation to put the interests of the bondholders before those of the public or the workers whom it employs. Moreover, all these bodies have been created too much in the image of private capitalist business, with the result that they both enjoy too much immunity from ministerial direction in terms of any public economic plan, and fail to make any change in the status of their employees, or to provide for any element of "workers' control".

These defects can, however, be rectified; and, subject to what has been said, the Public Board or Corporation is the appropriate model for industrial reorganization. What is valuable in it is, above all else, that it does provide for disinterested management, and does in practice give the technician a higher status and influence than he generally enjoys in private, profit-making concerns. What is needed is to add to this on the one hand a more effective co-ordinating control over policy by means of a State organization for concerted economic planning, and on the other a real participation by the workers in control, not merely by putting trade-union leaders on to the governing Board or Commission but—what is much more important—by giving the fullest recognition to workshop machinery effectively representing the actual working groups.

All this must be, in the main, a matter of post-war reconstruction; for we cannot here and now create definitive Public Corporations for the control of the essential industries and services. We can, however, create machinery which will prepare the way for this new order in industrial affairs. We can, to begin with, give every encouragement to the shop stewards' movement which is now rapidly gaining strength in the war factories. In the last war this movement, frowned upon almost equally by the State, the employers, and the officials of the trade unions, was driven into opposition, and played, save here and there, no constructive rôle in increasing war output. To-day the situation is very different. The trade unionists in the workshops are not resisting the dilution of labour, but keenly supporting it. The shop stewards, instead of regarding with suspicion every invasion of established trade-union customs, are pressing for more, wherever they see a chance of increasing war output. Their complaint now, despite long hours, is not that they are being driven too hard, but that their services are not being employed fully enough, or to the best purpose. They are eager to co-operate in and with management in order to increase production.

This situation offers a marvellous chance of introducing a large instalment of real workers' control into the factories. But this chance will not be taken advantage of without a large alteration in the attitudes of the great majority of managers and high business officials. The representatives of capital investment are for the most part hostile to an increase in the power of the trade unions; and this attitude is largely shared by the professional managers and technicians, or at all events by the older men among them. Nor is this attitude likely to change as long as the managerial grades continue to regard themselves as the representatives of capital, and to think of the private owners of the business, rather than of the business itself, as paying them their salaries. If they, in common with the manual workers, became the employees of the State, and if, further, their new master gave them positive direction that the public policy was one of close collaboration with the workers and encouragement of workshop organization, many of them would speedily change their tune and come to think of themselves as co-partners with the manual workers in the conduct of the factory and no longer as watchdogs for the capitalist class, with a mission to bark at every move in the direction of industrial democracy.

There would be, no doubt, many industrial managers who would find this change of front difficult, and some who would bitterly resent it. There are many such instances now, even in face of the very mild disapproval which the Minister of Labour ventures to express of firms which still refuse to recognize trade unionism or to admit any rights of collective bargaining on the part of their employees. But I believe the majority of managers would settle down fairly readily to the new conditions; and I feel sure the consequence would be to raise output and to improve substantially the average quality of industrial management.

At the other end of the scale, the changes I have put forward would involve that the State would deal in future, about matters of war production, not with the financial directors of big businesses but with the actual managers of particular factories. The financial element would retire to a back seat, and the technicians and factory administrators would move up to the front. The Regional Boards of the Production Executive would become focusing-points for the concerted tackling of local and regional problems of production over a much wider field than now; and the entire control of war industry would be envisaged much more in technical and much less in financial terms. All the troubles arising out of " cost plus " contracting and other objectionable methods of settling up financially between the State and the big employers would disappear, and would be replaced by a proper form of scrutiny of real, as distinct from financial, costs. For real, and not financial, costs are what really matter.

I am convinced that this point is of the first importance. The trouble about production to-day is not only that there is a continual clash between public and private interests, but also that financial and technical considerations are perpetually getting muddled up. What really matters in wartime is not money cost but real cost—the amounts of scarce man-power, materials and machine-time that are getting used up in producing a given result. But this way of thinking, familiar to the technician and the production engineer, is altogether unfamiliar both to the Treasury and the Civil Service generally and to the financial mind which is apt to dominate big business. To get the financiers and the Civil Servants out of the key positions, and to bring technically minded persons in, is an object as worthy of attention as the taking of the profit motive out of war.

I come, then, to the assertion that, in order to get war production efficiently organized, we must set about doing four things.

First, we must take over the big factories, the mines, the transport system, and the other key positions, and for the war period eliminate from them every vestige of the profit motive and of control by the representatives of those who own the invested capital.

Secondly, we must do this without substituting bureaucracy for profiteering—that is, in such a way as to put control, under general government direction of policy, in the hands of technicians and professional business managers and not of Civil Servants.

Thirdly, we must enlist, much more positively than now, the services of the actual workers and their workshop representatives as participants in the tasks of wartime organization.

Fourthly, we must leave the question of the future ownership and control of industry to be settled as a matter of post-war policy, and must not allow considerations arising out of this matter to deflect us from our determination to get the wartime organization of production on the most efficient lines that we can contrive.

These are the tasks which lie immediately before us : if we concentrate upon them, we can avoid the peril, in which we now are, of making our people weary, not from overwork, but from the consciousness of wasted resources and of standing around doing nothing, when there is so much to be done, because of bad organization and divided counsels. In this way, and in no other that I can see, shall we get a workable industrial plan, and be in a position to wage total economic war, not only without sacrificing our democracy, but in such a way as to enlist the democratic forces in industry on the side of victory.

## 2. EQUALITY OF SACRIFICE
### *by* FRANCIS WILLIAMS

I BEGIN by exercising an author's privilege to quarrel with a title chosen for him by someone else. It is, I think, high time we expunged the phrase equality of sacrifice from our vocabulary. It is a tired phrase with the edges blurred. And it sets altogether the wrong tone for our discussions.

My objection to this phrase does not arise out of any objection to equality. On the contrary, I am passionately anxious for greater equality. Nor does it come from an objection to the idea of sacrifice. Great sacrifices will clearly be necessary if we are to win this war and establish a true democracy after it. But when we talk, or think, in terms of equality of sacrifice, we seem to me to be looking at our problems from the wrong angle. The emphasis is on sacrifice when it ought to be on opportunity, indeed, on something even more positive than opportunity, on the privilege of helping forward the great purposes of democracy.

We have, I think, to bring to bear on the problems of democracy during and after this war a quite different social attitude from that of the past if we are to make democracy the living creed which the perils and opportunities of the time invite. Trotting out the old tired phrase of equality of sacrifice does not seem to me to do that.

When there is need for volunteers for particularly hazardous work in one of the services—for the submarine service, shall we say—the call that is made, and that is always answered, is not made and certainly is not answered in any spirit of arithmetical calculation as to the equality of sacrifice involved. On the contrary, it is made and answered as an invitation to participate in a great opportunity. Now it seems to me very essential that this quite common attitude towards the possible or indeed probable sacrifice of one's life in the national cause shall be widened to embrace the sacrifice of property and privilege if there is to be any assurance of progress towards a more complete democracy.

It is a very odd and, I think, important fact that there is a quite general agreement in all sections of the community that when the sacrifice of life is in question, then equality of sacrifice is the right and natural thing. But when it comes to the question of sacrificing possessions and power, particularly power, the matter takes a different turn. It seems to me, as I say, an odd and interesting thing that this should be so. I cannot seriously conceive that the kind of sacrifices of social and economic privilege that are necessary to make our society more truly democratic can represent for any sensible person " a fate worse than death "—to use a phrase which once, I believe, filled the heroines of popular novels with terror, although it appears merely to excite anticipation in the breasts of most of the young ladies who grace the pages of the popular literature of to-day.

Economic and social equality ought not, it seems to me, to represent for any sane person a fate worse than death. Yet many of us frequently act as if it did.

Consider, for example, what happens if one suggests that in financing this war it might be worth while establishing an income ceiling of, shall we say, a net two thousand pounds a year. Two thousand pounds a year is not great wealth, but it certainly is not penury. Yet immediately such a proposition is advanced it is denounced on the grounds that it would involve so vast an upset of personal commitments entered into by the people with incomes above that amount, that it could not be seriously considered either as a matter of economic equality or financial expediency. But nobody for one moment ever dreams of suggesting that everybody with an earned income of above £2,000 a year shall be exempt from service in the armed forces because of the breaking of personal commitments of one kind or another which would result from them ceasing to earn their former incomes. Nobody suggests that, and if any one did the people would rise in righteous wrath and throw him into the nearest pond amidst the applause of Parliament and Press. No one suggests it because service in the armed forces is tied up in the public mind with the risk of life, and there is a very sound social convention that in accepting that risk there shall be equality. But when a comparable proposition is put forward on the level of democratic desirability, quite a different attitude of mind comes into being.

Now, I am much more interested in trying to discover why there is this different attitude of mind and whether we can change it, than I am, at this particular moment, in providing a kind of actuarial assessment of what ought to be done to produce a genuine equality of sacrifice. I believe if we can change this attitude, then there is some hope that genuine equality of sacrifice will follow. If we do not succeed in changing it, then all the careful arithmetical calculations in the world—and I have been guilty of several in my time—will produce nothing at all, however reasonable and logical they may be.

But first let us look for a moment at some of the facts of inequality as it exists in Britain. I am not very enamoured of statistics in public lectures. When they are reliable they are apt to be old and dull, and when they are new and startling they are often unreliable. But the really startling thing about these facts that I am going to quote is that they are all well known. They represent eight facts of inequality in this country—eight quite common facts. The list could be extended to eighty or eight hundred, but these eight will do for a beginning. Here they are :

*Fact No.* 1. The infantile death-rate in Glasgow is one hundred and nine per thousand. In the pleasant and prosperous county of Surrey it is forty-two per thousand. In Hertfordshire it is thirty-eight per thousand.

*Fact No.* 2. Eleven thousand babies now die every year who would be saved if the infantile death-rate throughout all Britain could be brought down to the level of the comfortable Home Counties.

*Fact No.* 3. Fifty-four thousand people of all ages would be saved from death every year if the death-rate, age for age, in industrial areas such as South Wales, Lancashire, Yorkshire and Durham, was brought down to the level existing in the Home Counties.

*Fact No.* 4. For every baby that died shortly before the war of pneumonia and bronchitis in middle-class homes, five hundred and seventy-two babies died in poor homes.

*Fact No.* 5. Thirty per cent. of our population, or approximately sixteen million people, had, before the war, less to spend on food than was required to purchase the minimum B.M.A. diet regarded as necessary to maintain health.

*Fact No.* 6. Eighty per cent. of the total capital wealth of Britain belongs to six per cent. of the people.

*Fact No.* 7. Of the twelve million families in Britain eight million have as their total savings—as their total guard, that is, against future disasters—less than £100. Half of that eight million have less than £2. The entire property of most of this bottom four million consists merely of what they stand up in and of a few sticks of furniture.

*Fact No.* 8. Although because of a substantial rise in the total national wealth the standard of living of what are known as the working classes has risen considerably over the past hundred years, the share of the total national wealth going to wage earners has actually fallen, not risen, during the past three-quarters of a century. It had fallen from fifty-five per cent. in 1860 to forty per cent. just before the war. Inequality had increased, not decreased.

Well, there are eight facts. The significant thing about those facts, I repeat, the thing that I want you to remember about them, is that they are not new facts. They are well-known facts. They have been written about and talked about again and again. They are the sort of facts that we all know and that those of us who are Fabians and have therefore a congenital itch that way write pamphlets about.

But nothing very much gets done about them.

During the six months of heavy bombing last year, nearly twenty-four thousand people were killed. If the bombing had gone on at that rate for twelve months, forty-eight thousand people would have been killed. That would have been six thousand less in the twelve months than die every year in this country from perfectly preventable causes, judging by the statistical difference between the death-rate in the poor areas and the comfortably-off areas.

We all got extremely excited and angry about the deaths from bombing, but we hardly disturb ourselves at all about the larger number of deaths from preventable causes in peace time.

When a ship taking children from Britain to the United States was torpedoed and sunk by the Germans, we were all very rightly horrified at this further evidence of the brutality of the Nazi regime, which considers the torpedoing and murdering of children as part of the tactics of war. When we are told that eleven thousand British babies in poor districts die every year who need not die, we are not in the least bit horrified by our own brutality.

If on that torpedoed ship of evacuee children going to America the middle-class and comfortably-off children had been carefully packed into the lifeboats first and taken to safety and the poor children had been allowed to drown, a great surge of anger and horror would have swept across the country and across the whole world. But there is no surge of anger and of horror when we know that in peace time thousands of poor children are allowed to die who would live if they were born in middle-class and comfortably-off families.

Now it does not seem to me that there is much point in drawing up nicely balanced plans for equality of sacrifice and carefully worked out budgetary systems for producing that equality so long as this state of mind exists.

Unless and until the facts of inequality in peace time have as big an impact on our social conscience as they would do if they were translated into the terrain of death by violence and war, all the calculations in the world will not produce real results. The indignation that stirs us if we hear of inequality in one sector must stir us if there is inequality in any sector.

Why does it not do so? Why is there this difference? Why is it that when there is the call to sacrifice of life in war there is an immediate readiness on the part of all to accept—nay, to demand—that it shall be answered equally by all, but that when the call to equality comes in the less violent spheres of social living it is bitterly and implacably opposed?

We are, or claim to be, a democratic nation. Certainly we are ready to fight to the death for certain aspects of democracy. Now the basic ideas of democracy have never been better expressed than in the American Declaration of Independence. A cardinal feature of that Declaration is its insistence that all men are born equal. Yet in our practical application of democracy and in our social attitude to the problems of democracy, we insist, nay, we are ready to go to the stake to defend, the sacred right to inequality. In theory, democracy is a great equalitarian creed; in practice, inequality is its chosen wear, except when it comes to dying in war. Why is this?

The kind of sacrifices that war requires—or rather that it used to require for modern war, often requires new sacrifices quite different from those of the past—are hallowed by tradition. They have behind them the backing of a strong social code and the massive influence of an extremely successful educational system. I mean by this the Public School system. I am not one of those who laugh at the Public School system. I have too high a respect for its success in achieving its objects. The privileged classes who established and have maintained the Public Schools were, and are, well aware of a fact which too often escapes the attention of " progressives ", although it has not escaped that of Hitler. It is that if you wish securely to establish a social system you must so educate its members that acceptance of the obligations and sacrifices required to maintain it becomes second nature to them.

The Public School system is based on the twin conception of privilege and sacrifice; the privilege which accrues to those trained as members of a leader class, the sacrifices necessary to maintain the dominance of that class. Consider how substantial the sacrifices required by the Public School system and gladly accepted by its disciples are. It would be unfair to believe that parental affection exists less strongly among the fathers and mothers of what are known as the upper and upper-middle classes than it does among those of what are called the middle and lower classes. To suggest so would, I am sure, be untrue. At least I hope it would. Yet the parents of these classes have for many years accepted an abdication of the delights of parenthood such as would appal middle-class and poor parents, such as indeed these latter have accepted only with the very greatest reluctance —and not always even then—under the compulsion of air raids. These " privileged " parents have consistently, and as a matter of course, accepted separation from their children at the tenderest age and sent them when they were scarce out of their toddlers' clothes to live at preparatory boarding-schools, from whence they could pass in due course without pause to their public schools, to be trained from their earliest years in the business of making a privileged society work. Now the successful operation of a privileged society, and particularly the maintenance of such a society, on a comparatively stable basis over a long period of years is not a simple matter. It requires a great deal of tact, judgment and political sense on the part of the privileged so that their privilege, while soundly assured, shall not be so blatant, so obviously ill deserved or so clearly lacking in the justification of any service rendered, as to incite the unprivileged to revolt.

On the whole, the privileged classes of Britain have been remarkably successful in this. They have managed to maintain an unequal society with, on the whole, as election results show, the acquiescence of most of those who suffer most under such a system. This has been done partly by allowing there to be a certain number of ways by which the most active and intelligent of the under-privileged, who might otherwise have used their energies to attack privilege, can themselves climb to a privileged position. The stairway from the somewhat squalid surroundings of the basement up to the solid comfort of the first floor, and from there up to the ease and luxury of the top story has not been a particularly broad or easy stairway, but it has been climbable. The society at the top has not made the mistake of being absolutely rigid and exclusive. It has been prepared to absorb new members, singly or, when there has been a shift in economic power such as that which flowed from the industrial revolution, in large numbers. It has preferred to absorb the thrusting new-comers rather than to fight them for possession, and in that it has been wise to its own interests.

But this willingness to open its ranks to the successful is only half, although an important half, of the story. At the same time the privileged classes in Britain have been shrewd enough to recognize that the most stable foundation for privilege is a tradition of service to the community. The Public Schools have been, within their limitations, the guardians and inculcators of that tradition. Because the society they existed to maintain was an imperialist society, their tradition was one suitable to imperialism. It naturally included the military virtues among which there ranks high the obligation to set an example in dying to those beneath one. As a consequence the Public School-educated privileged classes of Britain have held to their privilege in all things but this. Here they have sought equality of sacrifice, although in all other things they have fought it. They may have been determined to live like greedy boys, but they were usually ready to die like gentlemen.

This Public School tradition which sponsored this readiness to sacrifice one's life—but not one's property— for the community and which has affected much more than the public schools themselves, permeating our whole educational system was in its way and its time a great tradition. But it was never of course a democratic tradition. It was a tradition founded on inequality which is why it took the shape it did.

I said earlier that those who founded it were fully alive to the fact that if you wish securely to establish a social system you must so educate its members that the acceptance of the obligations and sacrifices required to maintain it becomes second nature to them. Those who believe in an equalitarian democracy do not seem to me to have been nearly so alive to that fact as the Public Schools, nor nearly so alive to it as have a very different but not less realist thinking group, the communist leaders of the U.S.S.R.

It has become clear with the German attack on Russia that the people of the Soviet during the last twenty years or so have acquired a feeling of loyalty to their society at once logical and passionate. They have been in no doubt as to the meaning of equality of sacrifice, nor that when great issues are at stake the opportunity of sacrifice should be looked upon as a privilege. When they are called upon to scorch their earth, to burn their houses, to destroy their crops, no question of distinction between one kind of sacrifice and another comes into *their* minds. They are ready to sacrifice not merely their lives but everything. Twenty years of education in the purposes of their society have given them a standard of values that puts material possessions and personal property in the right perspective.

I believe British democracy even in its present incomplete state has great qualities which Russian communism does not possess. But Russian communism appears to have succeeded in arousing a spirit of convinced devotion among its people greater, at any rate in the sphere of property and privilege, than the democracies have yet succeeded in arousing. Unless democracy can arouse a comparable emotion, then I doubt whether it will survive the war or will have much right to survive the war.

In its beginnings democracy was a great social revolutionary movement. It represented an immense affirmation of the importance of the common man. That tremendous faith in the equality of man which sounds so nobly in the Declaration of Independence was at its heart. I do not of course want to pretend that the people who fought the democratic revolution and who broke the strength of the old regime of autocracy were thinking in terms of absolute equality for everybody. Democracy came into being very largely out of the efforts and energies of energetical, practical and enterprising men who wanted to be sure of freedom of opportunity to exercise their own abilities and who found it necessary to break the barriers which stood in the way of the exercise of those abilities. They were primarily concerned with their own right to exercise their own abilities. But they were capable of seeing and of affirming that the equality of opportunity which they demanded for themselves ought to be available to all people. It is true that, as so often happens, their practice was very different from their theory—it is usually only very gradually that political practice catches up with theory. Nevertheless, the great move forward, the tremendous advance that the idea of democracy did make in the history of the world, was in its expression of the idea of the importance of the ordinary man; its belief in government of the people, instead of government of kings or soldiers or rich men.

To-day, the revolutionary movement of democracy is once again challenged by the old autocracy, this time in a new Nazi dress. In meeting that challenge it is very desirable that we should re-examine our own conceptions of democracy and particularly that conception of equality which is at its heart. I believe this to be necessary if we are to win this war in the most expeditious and forthright way open to us. It is certainly necessary if we are to have any genuine hope of establishing after the war the kind of society that will prevent us from falling into fresh wars. Foreign policies grow out of and are a development of home policies. It is hopeless to think that we shall achieve a good foreign policy of international agreement and federation and co-operation after the war out of a home policy based on the exact opposite of those qualities. Moreover, just as the foreign policies of peace grow out of home policies, so do the policies of war. The methods by which war is fought and the things people are prepared to sacrifice in its cause—these too grow out of and are a projection of home policy.

In this war so far there has been a considerable movement towards a greater financial equality, or rather a certain narrowing of the immense chasm which yawns between the very poor and the very rich. The rich have been heavily taxed and have accepted that taxation with very good grace. But they have only accepted it on the understanding that the sacrifices they are called upon to make now will safeguard their right to the advantages of inequality in the future.

It is not easy at the moment for anyone to receive a net income of more than £7,000 a year. I do not suggest that £7,000 is not a pleasant enough net income capable of relieving the head of the household of those worries about the rent which in normal times trouble so large a part of the population. But it is comparatively small beer compared with some of the great pre-war incomes. So far these financial sacrifices have been accepted without grumbling. But when discussion of sacrifice moves to the possibility of the permanent sacrifice of economic power, of capital possessions and of social prestige, then the situation is changed. Then, indeed, does the ship of progress find itself threatened by the solid rock of implacable opposition. And what is more, that opposition is composed not merely of the handful of the very rich but also of immense numbers of ordinary people who have been mis-educated into believing that there is some sacred virtue in economic and social inequality, instead of having been properly educated in the good democratic faith of equality.

Now I refuse to believe that men and women who are prepared to accept—nay, passionately embrace—the justice of equality of sacrifice of life, cannot be brought to accept the justice of equality in other and less important matters if they are inspired to a true understanding of the purposes of the democracy of which such equality is an essential part. The trouble with democracy is not merely that, as the cynical lady said of monogamy, everybody criticises it but no one will try it. It is also that we have not yet seriously begun to educate ourselves in the implications of the democratic idea.

Public School education has been based on a very clear appreciation of the social and economic implications of a privileged society and a very definite determination to produce the kind of people who can make such a society work. Communist education has been based on an equally clear appreciation of what is required of the citizens of a communist society. Nazism has designed its educational system to produce good fascists, and judging from the cruel and fanatical ruthlessness of the young German fighting man it has done its work well.

But democrats have not evolved an educational system which appreciates the implication of the democratic idea or understands the kind of social obligations that it is necessary for the citizen to accept if democracy is to work. Education for democracy is a much more difficult matter then is education to maintain economic and social privilege, or education for fascism or even education for communism, because democracy is a much more adult and revolutionary philosophy than any of these. But it is not an impossible task if those who believe in democracy really set their minds to it. The vistas which democracy opens are so vast, the values it seeks to establish are so noble and the call to human endeavour is so challenging, that I cannot believe that more than a handful of people would oppose the sacrifices it requires from the most privileged if they understood what was at stake. I may in this be taking an over-optimistic view of human nature, but when I see the immense sacrifices men and women are prepared to accept during war for a cause they understand, I cannot believe that I am. The difficulty is to get the understanding.

Unfortunately few of those who talk about democracy are much interested in education or they are only interested in its most superficial and politically exploitable aspects. It is a subject that but rarely, I fear, excites the politically minded and one that appears to offer few enticements to ambitious politicians of the Left. Yet it is, of course, quite fundamental to any sensible discussion of equality of sacrifice, fundamental because until men and women are educated to an understanding of the true democratic values no plan for equality produced by any of us will ever get anywhere.

I said earlier that democracy was the most revolutionary of all doctrines. Because that is true, education for democracy cannot be simply a matter of logic, although democracy has logic and reason firmly on its side. It must be a spiritual matter as well as a logical one. We shall achieve equality of sacrifice when men and women not only accept the fact that greater equality is reasonable but feel passionately that social inequality is unjust—as passionately as they now feel that when the great issues of life and death face men and women and children on board a torpedoed ship neither rank nor wealth shall be given preference.

    Until we generate that feeling all our well-meaning Fabian efforts to draw up new tracts for the times and to produce carefully prepared and logically unassailable plans for the reconstruction of this or that industry, admirable and necessary although those plans are, will have no affect. We have, in other words, somehow to raise this whole discussion of equality of sacrifice and of democracy and socialism, which is a part of democracy, from the plane of a purely intellectual explanation of why this or that method of running our economic affairs is better than that or this and give to it a new spiritual force and meaning. We have to bring back to democracy some of the religious revolutionary fervour which it had in its beginnings. We have to create a new revolutionary dynamic of democracy. What do I mean by a revolutionary dynamic? I do not necessarily mean revolutionary in the sense of violence and civil war. I mean that driving force which is to be found at the heart of all successful revolutionary movements and without which they would never have succeeded : the will to establish what are judged to be the great principles that should guide action and to enforce those principles, whatever administrative or social difficulties may stand in the way. At this moment, especially, we need, I think, to review our society in the light of those great ideals of social justice out of which democracy was born. In those ideals there lives, awaiting a new release, a revolutionary dynamic that could make equality of sacrifice not something to be imposed upon an unwilling people, but a challenge gladly to be accepted. That at least is my conviction. That, it seems to me, is the most important work awaiting Socialists at this moment. I hope we shall be equal to it.

# 3. DEMOCRACY IN WAR TIME
## by HAROLD J. LASKI

### I

I MEAN by a democratic society something more than a society in which the holders of the state-power are chosen by universal suffrage. I mean also a society in which men and women are able to hold the great ends of life in common by their free choice. I mean a society in which the rule of law stands above the discretion of any individual, in which a breach of the law is certain to involve the responsibility of the offender. I mean a society in which the expression of thought is free unless it can be shown by the classic procedure we have evolved through centuries that such expression is a source of grave and imminent danger to the society's existence. I mean a society in which the title to privilege is based upon reason and not upon prescription ; and I mean by privilege the receipt of a dividend from social effort without a corresponding personal contribution to the common stock. In a democracy men and women are ends as well as means ; those who exercise power apply its authority for purposes made valid by the approval, given without constraint, of ordinary people. A democracy is known by the rights that it maintains ; and the more equal the opportunity to enjoy those rights the more full and real is the democracy. The aim of democratic government is freedom ; but there is no effective freedom in a society if there are wide differences between citizens in their access to the good things of life. By the good things of life I mean economic security, health, leisure, and an education which makes possible the enjoyment of the intellectual heritage of civilization.

So much is necessary in preamble, if the nature of my argument is to be understood. The Britain which entered this war was only very partially democratic. Great privileges were enjoyed by a few without the possibility of rational justification. Millions of people, through no fault of their own, had no economic security, poor health, inadequate education, a leisure, therefore, where they had it, from which the prospect of dignity or creativeness was too often absent. What our democracy was on the eve of the war has just been painted for us in unforgettable pages by Mr. Seebohm Rowntree ! It was still a society marred by the worship we have so long offered to the religion of inequality. It was still a society in which the comfort of the few was purchased by the sufferings of the many. It was still a society in which social and economic changes, the validity of which was capable—look at the single realm of nutrition—of scientific demonstration, were fought with all the power and ingenuity privilege can muster in its defence. Britain in 1939 paid lip-service to the ideal of a democratic society. It had not begun to seek, in a radical way, to give its formal faith deliberate and conscious translation into the daily lives of its citizens.

It was a Britain still divided into Disraeli's two nations of the rich and the poor ; I add a nation on the threshold of differences more profound than any by which our people have been divided since the days of Chartism. It was a Britain in which men lived so differently that they were in danger of thinking too differently to be able to maintain the great ends of life in common. The masses deeply moved by the spectacle, amid all its faults, of the Russian Revolution and its achievements ; the ruling class with so little abhorrence of Fascism in Italy and Nazism in Berlin that they could not see, or refused to emphasize, the grim tyranny inherent in both. It was a

Britain which did not know the depth of the dangers by which it was confronted, dangers internal as well as external; which had held so long a position of unchallengeable supremacy that it had almost forgotten the ancient truth that freedom is won by sacrifice and maintained only by magnanimity. For—let us be honest about it—there was little magnanimity in the period of appeasement; and the forces which sacrificed China and Abyssinia, Austria and Albania, Czechoslovakia and Spain, were the same forces that, confronted by the need to reshape the foundations of their own society, preferred their private privilege to public justice. In part, at least, the roots of this war lie in our unwillingness to achieve democracy at home. For those who are uninterested in domestic justice will hardly recognize the enemies of freedom abroad until their own privilege is directly threatened.

Munich was in one sense a disaster. In another, it was a crowning mercy. For it awakened, if at an immense price, alike our rulers and the people to the understanding that their right as a people to shape their own destiny had been put in final hazard. It reminded them that if they had important differences, they had also not less vital identities. It compelled them to the recollection that if they had great problems to solve, they had also great traditions to preserve. Against our British way of life I should not deny that a formidable indictment can be drawn. But I should argue that, however formidable, on balance what Abraham Lincoln called the "common people" in this country live under institutions which give them a hope of self-fulfilment at least as great as that enjoyed in any other country; infinitely greater than the hope of any other people save those of the Soviet Union and the United States of America. Our social and economic inequalities were grave; increasingly, the masses were becoming aware that they had the power, not less than the right, to seek their redress. We maintained religious freedom. We had a tolerance for ideas the greatness of which appears the more remarkable the more deeply we ponder the tragic spectacle of Europe. We had a judiciary which was, if not unbiased, at least beyond corruption. We had a Parliament which, with all its defects both of composition and procedure, knew how to discuss great issues greatly; if, as I believe, the right to oppose is of the essence of democratic government, our Parliamentary system offers a foundation upon which, with good will—the condition is important—a democratic society can be built. Our Civil Service, if it lacked imagination and, as the war was to show, the capacity for audacious innovation, was more honest and more competent than any comparable bureaucracy. The armed forces of the State had no separate interest in its functioning; it would never have occurred to their leaders—the fact is of the utmost significance—to question the supremacy of the civil power. As a whole, our system was a compromise between democracy in the political realm—itself a very recent development in our history—and an economic power oligarchically organized which was in its turn related to a certain aristocratic vestigia still able to influence profoundly the habits of our society. The virtue of the system was that it still left elbow-room—though not too much elbow-room—for that give and take which enables men to settle their differences by discussion and not by machine-guns. I add that the system was built upon the possession of a vast colonial empire about the condition of which we had at least the decency to be increasingly ashamed. For Socialists, at any rate, are aware that those who perpetuate injustice in Allahabad or Jamaica or Southern Rhodesia will not hasten to redress it in Glasgow or in Manchester.

I speak as an Englishman of a race which found a refuge from oppression in this country three hundred years ago, and of a faith alien in its ritual, though not, I add, in its ethic, from the traditional creed of this country. I speak of Britain, therefore, with an inevitable detachment. I have lived in many countries. Nowhere have I found in greater degree either the qualities which make private life lovely or in public relations the instinctive embodiment of the anxiety for fair play. I know that there are special reasons for these things—not least that geographical isolation which science has only destroyed in my own lifetime. I should admit the truth of much of the indictment Matthew Arnold drew up against the British people—its excessive reliance upon the cash nexus as a bond between men; its worship of respectability and convention; its retention of the aristocratic belief that ideas are unimportant because a final bargain has been made with history. Most of what Marx and Lenin said in scorn of Labour politicians and trade-union leaders is true. Yet when all is said against this people that can be said, British leadership seems to me to have been a beneficent thing in the history of civilization.

It has given the world, I think, certain things the splendour of which becomes the more evident the more starkly we contemplate the implications of alternative leadership. First, there has been a general and genuine refusal to inflict pain for the sake of inflicting pain; where there have been exceptions to this rule, as in Ireland or India or Africa, it is a body of our own citizens who have been foremost in protesting against them. Second, there has been an intuitive understanding that the well-being of a people is born of the compromises of experience and not of the ruthless logic of ideas, so that British administration has, in general, been marked by a massive common sense which usually recognizes the danger signals in time; it has been felt, perhaps, rather than known, how right Burke was when he insisted that prudence is the first of the political virtues. And, thirdly, the British people is not a people that has nursed resentments; it knows how to be generous even to the beaten foe. Here I pray in aid, as the lawyers say, our treatment of Germany in the inter-war years. I ask any honest observer to compare that treatment with Germany's behaviour to the countries Hitler has conquered; I am prepared to have Britain judged by the comparison. Or compare the danger our statesmen are prepared to run from a neutral Eire with the implications of Hitler's attack on Norway or the Low Countries. There is, with all its blunders and crimes—I do not deny the reality of either—an abiding sense in the people of this country that power, national power and international power, must be subject to rule which is the inherent and inescapable condition of civilized living. The British citizen may be poor, he may be half-educated, he may lack the vivacity of the Italian, the thoroughness of the German, the clarity of mind which seems a French inheritance; but he does not forget that he is a man, and his humanity leads him to insist that manhood is a title to rights. So long as he has a chance of moulding the world to that pattern, it may retain its freedom. Only by that retention can it attain the status of a democratic society.

2

You may think that I have wandered from the theme I have been given. In reality, I have come to its core. For my central argument is that what is threatened in war time is the peculiar set of conditions which made British leadership in modern times a source of liberation not less than an instrument of authority, a technique of freedom as well as a strategy of power. I want to discuss the two things which seem to me to arise from this view : first, the question of whether, in the political realm, we have maintained the conditions which made our world-leadership tolerable to all save the aggressor-nations, and, second, whether we are, in the necessary measure, adopting the procedures those conditions require to the immense demands the need for victory obviously makes upon them. For the demands are quite literally immense. Never in our history have we lived so nearly or so ominously in the very shadow of defeat. Never have we met an enemy the informing idea of whose purpose denied so ruthlessly those habits which we collectively call civilization. It is not only necessary for us to will what is right. It is also necessary for us to know what it is right to will.

I take first the realm of civil liberties. I observe, what it is vital to observe, that total war is not a graceful minuet but a dread gamble with death in which the independence of the nation is the stake in hazard. War means fear ; fear means insecurity ; insecurity is the prime enemy of reason and of tolerance. Granted this, I think the British record in this war is a remarkable one. There has been one unforgivable folly—the treatment of alien refugees. I regret the unlimited discretion given to the Home Secretary to maintain internment without judicial scrutiny ; if I may say so, Lord Atkin's dissent in *Liversidge* v. *Anderson* belongs to the noblest tradition of the Common Law. I admit fully the need for a full power to intern ; I say only that safeguards against its abuse could go further than those which have so far been created. There have been some bad police blunders in searches and seizures ; there have been some typical extravagances from the magisterial bench ; there have been typical follies on the part of the secret services, not least in the realm of military intelligence. I regard the manner in which the *Daily Worker* was suppressed as quite indefensible; and the Home Secretary seems to me to have made a poor show in defending its continued suppression while he continues to permit the weekly venom of that journal which so curiously calls itself *Truth*. I note, also, that there have been some bad blunders in the treatment of conscientious objectors, though, compared with the last war, that treatment has been on a remarkably higher level.

But add all this up, and see it in proportion to the dangers we confront, to the fact that there have been hours in which we did not know whether we should escape invasion, and I think a sober observer is bound to conclude that the degree to which the traditional civil liberties have been maintained is notable indeed. All the stupidities of the Ministry of Information, and, I add, of the successive Ministers of Information, have not gagged the press; the *Manchester Guardian* remains the *Manchester Guardian*, the *Evening Standard* and the *Times* have made vital criticisms with the emphasis they require, the weeklies, and especially the *New Statesman* and the *Tribune*, have written in the great tradition of a free press, perhaps I may be permitted to add, writing for a socialist public, that the editorial columns of the *Daily Herald* and *Reynold's* have constantly displayed the courage and persistance which are necessary to the maintenance of free government. The B.B.C., I admit, has been mostly like a timid maiden aunt anxious not to be known for the possession of any positive views. But, all in all, I think it is true to say that none of us who realizes what is at stake has felt seriously frustrated in the realm of opinion. I observe, at least, that until 22 June, 1941, members of the British Communist Party were left unimpeded to explain to America the unworthiness of our cause. Pacifism has hardly suffered interference as an organized movement. There has been little interference, save by Hitler, with the right of meeting. We have been occasionally angered, sometimes irritated, twice, I think, apprehensive. In the sum of it all, we remain free to comment much as we will, either in the spoken or in the written word.

I turn from this aspect to Parliament and the War Cabinet. This is more difficult and more contentious ground. A government in wartime is pretty certain to be immune from many of the dangers its mistakes will involve in peace. The power to refuse debate is increased ; the use of secret sessions tends to become a vicious habit ; attendance of members grows slack, since it takes a grave disaster to jeopardize the existence of the Government ; and the absence of so many of the younger members with the forces has a profound effect on the climate of Parliamentary opinion. The virtual suspension of by-elections, except for freak candidatures, by reason of the electoral truce, means, moreover, that the best way we have of making the Cabinet aware of the drift of public feeling is unavailable. Roughly speaking, a War Parliament sacrifices about one-third of its effective spirit to the exigencies of the time.

I do not deny that there are compensations. Any legislature develops, if it is permitted to speak at all, the habit of criticizing the executive ; that is both its principle and its inclination. It is, I think, true to say of this House that it remains admirable in the expression of grievance ; that on vital occasions, Narvik, for instance, or Crete, or supply, its debates have maintained the great tradition. The little knot of members, interestingly composed of all parties, who have devoted their energies to thorough-going attack on the Government in matters of major importance have had a real influence in the House and in the country. The work of the Select Committee on National Expenditure has been a very salutary check on administration ; here, as elsewhere, publicity is a healing grace. I note with interest that those members of the House who do not supinely follow the Party whips get, if not office, at least an audience in the country which the professional party hacks cannot secure. The situation seems to me to be fairly summarized by saying that the House of Commons always sets limits to the margins of governmental error by its very existence, and that where the error, as with the Chamberlain Government, is widely felt to be abysmal, the House remains the most vital element in our political safety. The debate which made Mr. Churchill Prime Minister will, I suggest, live in the text-books as a supreme example of the virtue of free institutions.

The difficulties of political democracy do not seem to me to lie predominantly in the Parliamentary realm in war time, but outside it in the realm of administration. There are certain things it is impossible not to note with alarm—the immense centralization of power in the hands of the Prime Minister, the consequent reduction of men who ought to be colleagues to a status more akin to that of under-secretaries, the tendency of problems, accordingly, to get neglected unless they can be brought effectively to the Prime Minister's notice. I do not think the remedy for this is the fashionable argument that we need a smaller war cabinet of men freed from departmental duties ; that is the illusion which does not understand the necessary relation of policy-making to administration. I recognize that Mr. Churchill is a very great War Minister—the greatest, I think, this country has known since Chatham. But, frankly, there are sides of life either hardly known to him, for example, the economic realm, in which he speaks like a skilful lawyer from a brief with which he is unfamiliar, or in which, as with India and the place of propaganda in the war effort, his prejudices blind him to the urgent reality. Of course, any society must pay a price for its great statesmen. I am not confident that some of his colleagues, especially his Labour colleagues, have used the authority which is theirs to insist—I ask you to note that word—that Mr. Churchill bring his great gifts of heart and head to the reconsideration of issues upon which he keeps his mind firmly closed. I am disturbed by the unhappy loss of the art of resignation; otherwise, clearly enough, we should either have had a new Minister of Mines or a new policy for the mines. I should have liked Mr. Grenfell to remember that it was resignation which gave Mr. Eden his status with the common people. The principle does not stop with Mr. Grenfell. Mr. Churchill is as near indispensability to the nation as any Prime Minister in the record. But, sometimes, I should have liked a more confident sense in the Labour leaders that they are hardly less indispensable to Mr. Churchill.

I have no time to dwell, as I should wish, on the implications for democracy of local government in war time. I must confine myself to two brief observations. First, the more carefully the work of appointed Commissioners is scrutinized, the stronger becomes the case for the elective system; and, secondly, whatever reasons operate to prevent parliamentary elections in wartime seem to me invalid in the local sphere. It is not only that their absence has resulted in caucus government on far too wide a scale; it is also that civil defence work has thrown up a reservoir of new and important organizing ability in local areas which ought to be made available for the general handling of local problems.

All this must be related to one aspect of politics in the war effort that has more importance, I think, than is generally assumed: I mean the aspect of appointments to administrative posts important enough to enable their holders to influence policy. The character of these, very largely, I do not say entirely, conforms to the view that posts which involve control belong naturally to the upper middle class and the aristocracy, while the tasks of the subordinates may be filled by people chosen from the rest of the community. It is, I submit, difficult not to be troubled by the way in which the war-time controls are full of business men whose interest in their future makes a singleness of allegiance by no means easy. It is difficult not to be troubled by the way in which the possession of a title has been a help to an important position; at one stage, the commissioned ranks of the A.T.S. and the Home Guard read rather like an extract from Debrett. There is a good deal of rather unhappy evidence to suggest that even a really competent person with left views had less chance of having his services accepted than one with influential backing who began to suspect the wisdom of the Munich settlement shortly after the fall of the Chamberlain Government.

I emphasize this aspect because, whatever the policy a government may pursue, its power to give effect to that policy depends very largely upon the instruments it selects for the purpose. Army education, for example, is not going to produce, and is not producing, a tithe of the influence it could produce if those in charge of it are afraid of the impact of political controversy upon the Army; I remind you that the strength of conviction in Cromwell's Ironsides was not wholly unconnected with their victory. Billeting is not going to be evenly administered if, as in one small borough I know, it is felt that the owners of great houses ought not to be inconvenienced by the presence of slum-dwellers from London. The full opportunities of war-time education will not be utilized if the Board of Education assumes that what great public schools like St. Paul's can do with a nobleman's country mansion, it is unable, in some mysterious way, to do for the secondary school children from bombed-out areas in London, or Manchester, or Merseyside.

In a word, men think differently who live differently. It is, I think, true to say that the historic composition of our Civil Service, on the one hand, and the predominant character of war-time appointments to its ranks, on the other, result in the assumption that the limits of possible experiment are far more narrow than they need to be. The standards set, the ends envisaged as permissible, are bounded by the ideas of a governing class of what is, broadly, suitable for its subjects. I think that is so in the field of consumption ; I think that is so in matters like the allowances to the dependants of the services ; I think it is the " inarticulate major premiss ", to use Mr. Justice Holmes' happy phrase, which underlies the pathetic inability of the Government to adopt a bold policy upon wages. Total war, whether we like it or not, is revolution ; and the main instruments the Government has chosen in the field of administration, while I do not doubt their zeal to wage the total war to victory, want, if it is at all possible, to evade the revolution. They believe too profoundly in what Mr. Churchill calls " traditional Britain ", in which, after all, their lives have fallen in rather pleasant places, to tamper, if they can help it, with the articles of faith of our religion of inequality.

### 3

That leads me to the concluding part of my analysis. We are fighting the most dangerous enemy our civilisation has ever known. Our power to beat him depends upon the maximisation of our productive effort. That, in its turn, depends upon our ability to maintain faith in those who, in the last analysis, feed and equip our fighting forces. Our ability to maintain that faith is a function of our power to convince the world that our declared ends in this war—democracy and freedom—are ends which, at all costs, we propose to achieve. Great perorations will not maintain that faith; nor will the prayerful vagueness which associates our effort with Christianity. Mr. Eden, I know, has used some fine phrases about the post-war period. There is even a Minister without Portfolio responsible for reconstruction. The country is littered with committees planning this and that and the other after victory has been won.

It is all grimly reminiscent of 1914–18; and I want to say with all solemnity that unless, before our victory, the word becomes the deed, the disillusion which will follow this war will be as profound as that which followed the last. I do not for a moment deny that there has been a number of small, but beneficent reforms in matters of social constitution. I agree that the status and the strength of the trade unions is higher than at any period in our history. But I am bound to point out three things. First, there has been no change in the fundamental character of economic power since 1939; its ownership remains broadly in much the same hands; its motives to effort are still, even in the context of war, geared to the over-riding principle of profit-making. Secondly, it is clear that the necessities of war-production have immensely strengthened the power of the big unit as against the small; without safeguards which depend upon the inner character of the post-war state—which will be set by its relations of production—the impact of those necessities may easily be in an anti-democratic direction. Thirdly, it is clear that the present compromise between *laissez-faire* and planned capitalism fails to give us either the coherency or the unity of direction which maximizes production. I do not know whether Sir John Wardlaw-Milne's famous estimate of production is right, or whether it should be eighty or even ninety per cent. of the potential. I do know that there is not a practical trade unionist in any vital industry who has not a grim tale of waste and inefficiency to tell; and a good deal of these are due to the desire of the Government to wage total war without making the revolutionary changes which are the necessary condition of victory.

It is here, I believe, that war builds the main threat to democracy. The change from war conditions back to peace conditions will be an immense operation. It will involve political adjustments, economic adjustments, psychological adjustments of a size and intensity we have never before known; and all of them will mean sacrifices from every vested interest in this country, trade-union interests, I add, not less than those of the employers. To-day, when the mood of the people is ready for sacrifice, prepared to welcome great experiment, it would be possible to organize the preparations for that change on a basis which would make the relations of production more proportionate to the forces of production. There has been no attempt by this Government to utilize that mood. The danger of this attitude is the obvious one that when the compulsion to unity and effort that the war imposes is withdrawn, men will seek, out of sheer fatigue and strain, to revert to their wonted routines in a world to which they have largely become irrelevant. I say with emphasis that we have got to begin now the organization of a revolution by consent or we shall drift, after the war, to a revolution by violence which will destroy the major ends for which we fight.

Capitalist democracy is an historic relationship which

persists by its power to secure expanding welfare for the masses without jeopardizing the privilege of the capitalist class. That power has disappeared; that is why the vested interests of Italy and Germany used Mussolini and Hitler as the executioners of democracy. That is why, also, until the very eve of the war they aroused so considerable an interest among those who lived by privilege. Our democracy, no doubt, is more deeply rooted than most others. But its survival depends, not less than theirs depended, upon its ability to use the State power to build relations which make possible expanding welfare. If reconstruction is not made a part of the actual process of organizing the war effort a psychological mood, a mental climate will have been lost which will never again be so favourable. And, more than this, the attempt to reconstruct after the war, with economic habits and institutions whose inner essence is hostile to the pledges we have given; hostile, to take one example only, to what is required to realize the Four Freedoms of which President Roosevelt has spoken so wisely—that attempt will lead inevitably to gigantic frustrations likely to jeopardize that temper of give and take in which alone the procedures of democracy retain their meaning. To make reconstruction a part of the process of maximizing the war effort now is to build the conditions for security when the war is over. Security is the secret of reason for it safeguards men from fear; and fear has always been the main enemy of freedom.

This, for me at least, is the central problem of the war. If we meet it with the courage and the intelligence it requires, we not only make certain our victory; we also make it certain that our victory is not thrown away. We give to the masses that hope and exhilaration which, it cannot be too often insisted, evoke the dynamic of democracy. We enable ourselves to keep the great ends of life in common ; thereby we buy time in which social justice may make terms with historic prescription. And by keeping the great ends of life in common here, we have our energies free to lead in the task of rebuilding Europe which, without our energies, may well find the chaos of the post-war period more grim and savage than the actual experience of war.

To face the problem of democracy in this way in war time itself, seems to me an obligation we owe to our allies not less than to ourselves. Above all, I venture to think, it is an obligation we owe to four peoples, to the Czechs and the Norwegians, to the Greeks and to the Russians. No scars are more honourable than those they bear ; not even our endurance and courage surpasses theirs. I do not deny that it is a very great thing to relieve them from the yoke of Hitlerism. I do deny that it is enough to relieve them from that yoke. Freedom from the external tyrant is only complete when the act of liberation creates the positive conditions in which a people can affirm its own essence. To that affirmation we have it in our power to make a unique contribution by setting, in the midst of war, an example of ordered social transformation to a system which, because it makes justice its objective, the world recognizes as an example to emulate.

That is the leadership it is in our power to give ; that is the only leadership which can justify the sacrifices this war exacts. We are obviously at one of the turning-points of history, not less surely than at the tidal wave we call the Reformation, or that other we call the French Revolution. Every element in our lives makes it clear that now, as then, a new society is struggling to be born, that the old order seeks to prevent its emergence. I wish we could make it known to our rulers that to be on the side of democracy means to be on the side of Revolution ; that to be, like Hitler, the symbol of hostility to democracy is to embody that principle of counter-revolution which, as he has so plainly shown, strips man of his humanity and takes him on the path to the jungle. We cannot will the end of democracy and freedom without willing the means. These are so clearly the planned utilization of our resources for the common good that, already, dependence upon the motive of private profit for the attainment of the common good seems like a contradiction in terms. Freedom depends upon economic security, and economic security depends upon common ownership. In these conditions an expanding welfare becomes possible which could make a cosmos of the international anarchy we have known. There is no other way to a peace that is enduring and creative.

This, I say, is what I wish we could make known to our rulers. They need not fear to call upon our people for sacrifice. We live in one of those periods in which the measure of his audacity is the test of the statesman. To safeguard democracy from its enemies means great experiment, large innovation, that kind of wisdom and courage which have made the name of Solon imperishable. I am not afraid to emphasize that it is precisely because this is a time of such grave danger, that it is our duty to make our socialist principles unmistakably heard.

> From the cloud comes the violent snow and the hailstorm, and the thunder springs from the lightning-flash. So from the men in power comes ruin to the state, and the people through their ignorance fall into the servitude of rule by one man. When a man has risen too high, it is not easy to check him after ; now is the time to take heed of everything.

So wrote Solon, in the first half of the sixth century before

Christ ; all history seems to me to offer proof of his words. "Now is the time to take heed of everything." To-morrow it may be too late. But if we act to-day, we may set our democracy on unbreakable foundations.

## 4. WOMEN AND THE WAR

### by MARY SUTHERLAND

How will the war affect the work and status of women? That question, so often asked, is asked only because women, politically emancipated since 1918, are not yet accepted as equal partners with men in the business of the community. Women won their political freedom in the upheaval of the last war, though they had to wait ten years—until 1928—to be given citizen rights on the same terms as men. So it is inevitable that there should be discussion as to whether this war's upheaval will accelerate their progress towards economic equality.

It is difficult for those who do not remember the pre-1914 world to measure the changes that have taken place in the position of women within a generation. Then they were entirely excluded from citizenship; denied recognition as human beings, though their exclusion was often defended on the sentimental ground that they were more than human beings—only a little, if at all, lower than the angels. Certain professions were barred to them; in others they were admitted reluctantly. In industry the range of their employment was narrower than to-day, and their labour was often sweated labour. More important than restrictions imposed by law were the prejudices and conventions which in every class decreed what a woman might, and might not, do. These conventions were, of course, bound up with the legal status of women, but they counted for more in the life of the individual woman.

Even before the law made her a citizen, the emancipating process had begun. Very early in the war the old hampering conventions began to go, as women in thousands put on uniform, or trooped into factories to do men's jobs, and to work side by side with men. It would be too much to say that the old prejudices had completely changed; but conditions had changed and prejudices were put in cold storage for the duration. From time to time in the period between two wars, they were taken out for an airing—in periods of acute depression they had a good run. But they never recovered their pre-1914 vitality.

This wartime experience of new work and new responsibilities led to a freedom and frankness and comradeship in the relations between men and women as workers and human beings, which was entirely new, and which must be counted among the emancipating influences as well as the fact of the vote.

Perhaps the most significant result of the new social and political freedom of women was the end of the women's movement, the feminist movement. It had been a great movement. Born in the passionate protest of Mary Wollstonecroft against the subjection of women at the close of the eighteenth century, it grew steadily in influence through the second half of the nineteenth century, drawing inspiration from the ideas which were shaping other movements for social justice and the liberation of the human mind; until it gathered all its forces for the stirring campaign for the vote in the years before the 1914 war. On the outbreak of war it suspended its activities. After the passing of the 1918 Act, it never revived.

This was hardly the result that many of the feminists who had gone into battle so gallantly in pre-war days had anticipated. Looking back, we can see now that it was an inevitable result. For the vote was not an end in itself—it was an instrument to secure other ends. Women, when they got the vote, wanted different things with it.

Perhaps the only true generalization that can be made about women is that they are like men in their variety and differences. They did not combine as women. They attached themselves to political parties according to their conception of the purposes for which the vote should be used. Those who were politically conscious realized that these purposes were not confined to what might fairly be described as " women's questions ". The vote gave them responsibility for *all* political questions ; for passing judgment on international policy as well as on the provision for maternity ; for securing—or denying—justice to an under-privileged class as well as to an under-privileged sex.

It must be noted, too, that the women's movement had been largely a middle-class movement. It is significant that Miss Eleanor Rathbone—whose work for women's emancipation puts us all in her debt—writing some years ago on the beginnings of the women's movement, quotes a passage from *Pride and Prejudice* where Charlotte Lucas reflects on her engagement to Mr. Collins :

> Her reflections were in general satisfactory. Mr. Collins to be sure was neither sensible nor agreeable ; his society was irksome and his attachment to her must be imaginary. But still he would be her husband. Without thinking highly either of men or matrimony, marriage had always been her object. It was the only honourable provision for well-educated women of small fortune, and however uncertain· of giving happiness, must be their pleasantest preservative from want.

That quotation indicates both the character and the limitations of the feminist movement. It was concerned to end the parasitic dependence of the women with small fortunes on their menfolk, and to win for them the right to work. It was not concerned with the thousands of women without small fortunes who knew about the right to work all too well. The right to work was a middle-class demand. To ask the vote as a means to win the right to work made little appeal to working-class women.

I am not suggesting that the vote meant nothing to working women. Of course it did. It raised their status as it raised the status of all women; through it they could help to free themselves from economic exploitation. But *their* emancipation was bound up with the cause of the whole working class. There could be no economic security and freedom for the great majority of women in a system which denied security and freedom to their fathers, husbands and brothers. Most of the brilliant leaders of the women's movement were blind to the wider implications of their demand for economic freedom, and so failed to win an enthusiastic following among working women.

This is not to underestimate what the women's movement accomplished nor what we owe to it. It is a reminder that the whole story of women's emancipation is not told in the history of the feminist organizations. For that we must look also to the organizations which championed the cause of the working woman, in shop, factory or the home. The sweated industries campaign, the fight for Trade Boards and the campaign for a Maternity Service are chapters in that story, as well as the struggle for the vote. All of us owe much for the improved status which women enjoy to-day, to women like Lady Dilke, Gertrude Tuckwell and Mary MacArthur, Margaret Llewelyn Davies and Marion Phillips, as well as to feminist leaders.

This is not the place to tell of the battle which the pioneers of the women's Trade Union Movement fought on behalf of the tens of thousands of women who had never needed to beg for the privilege of being allowed to work. It is worth remembering, however, that when a basic rate of 20*s*. a week for women workers in war factories was secured in 1916 after strenuous agitation by Mary MacArthur and the National Federation of Women Workers, it meant something like a revolution in women's wage standards ! Improvements that have taken place since then have been built on that foundation.

The status of women workers is still an inferior status. They are generally paid less than men for doing the same work. Wages for work done exclusively by women, even when it is skilled work, are less than the wages paid for unskilled men's work. An enquiry by the Ministry of Labour in 1940 in industries covering more than six million workers showed that the average earnings of women workers were rarely more than 50 per cent. of men's earnings, in many cases a good deal less.

Women have always been paid less than men—just because they are women. This is true of most professional work as of factory and other manual work. In every field of employment there are not only wages and salaries for various grades of work—there are also men's wages and women's wages, a wide gap between them.

There are two reasons why the double standard has persisted so long. It is accepted as just, on the ground that men have families to keep and women have not. This has never been true. Many women workers have dependants, many men have none. But as husbands and fathers are legally responsible for the maintenance of their wives and children, the discrepancy between men's and women's wages does not outrage most people's sense of justice. So long as there is no provision for child dependancy outside the father's wages, I believe it will not be possible to rally an effective public opinion behind the demand that men's wages and women's wages should alike be determined in relation to the value of the work and not to the sex of the worker.

The second reason is the weaker bargaining power of women. As Mary MacArthur put it—women are badly organized because they are badly paid and they are badly paid because they are badly organized.

The early trade unions, with a few exceptions like the textiles, were indifferent and sometimes hostile to admitting women. They were influenced by the traditional view that it was the proper destiny of a woman to be dependent on a man—her father or her husband. Some of them thought that women had no right to be in industry at all, that they were intruders there. This belief has no basis in fact. The work which women came into the factories to do was work which they had always done before the factory age in their homes. When the power machine killed home industry women followed their work to the mills. If we follow the progress of the old domestic industries through the machine age, it could as fairly be argued that men have been taking women's jobs from them, as that women have taken men's!

The unions, of course, saw in the low wages of women a constant threat to their own. It took years of discussion and experience to convince them that women would continue to be a menace to men's standards so long as they were outside the unions, completely unorganized. Even when that was realized, it was too readily assumed that it was hopeless to try to organize women. If Mary MacArthur and the Federation of Women Workers in the last war had only raised the wretched level of women's wages, it would have been a great achievement. But they did much more than that—they finally convinced the Trade Union Movement that women workers when organized were as determined to protect men's standards as to improve their own; that the conditions of men and women workers were bound up together ; and that it was *not* hopeless to try to organize the women.

The only sound basis for real equality of status is the principle of " the rate for the job ", a principle now generally accepted by the trade unions. This means, of course, that women should be paid the same rates as men where they are doing the same work. But " equal pay for equal work " is a phrase which has obscured the problem. Only a minority of women are doing the same work as men. There are " women's trades " and, within trades which employ both men and women, there is " women's work ". Women doing women's work are not paid " a rate for the job " but " a rate for the sex ", which has no relation to the skill or value of their work. Equal pay for equal work certainly ; but equality of status calls for a completely new approach to the methods by which payment for " women's work " is determined.

Two notable achievements of the trade unions since the war began are the agreements in the transport and engineering industries which give the women who are substituting men and doing men's work, after a probationary period, the men's rates. I think these agreements are likely to have far-reaching results not only by encouraging a more general application of the principle of " the rate for the job " wherever men and women are doing the same work, but by stimulating a new attitude to the problem of the different standards by which payment for men's work and women's work is determined. For women to work in a factory alongside men for half men's rates is a circumstance so usual as to be accepted all too readily without question ; for women to work for half men's rates alongside other women on men's rates is something new, which is likely to make women challenge the basis of their own wage standards and lead to a re-valuation of the whole field of " women's work ".

There is not only inequality in payment, there is also inequality of opportunity. Women have on the whole been excluded by custom from more skilled grades of work, and their opportunities for promotion have been limited. This is true of professional work as of industry and commercial employment. Women are rarely promoted to the highest posts even where in principle these are open to them.

The way to equality of status between men and women workers is through strong trade union organization. It is well known that women lag badly behind men in trade union strength, but two facts should be noted. The majority of women workers, prior to the war, were in occupations very difficult to organize—clerical and commercial work, domestic and personal service. The bulk of women trade unionists were in factory employment which represented only one-third of all occupied women.

Further, the majority of women workers are young, under twenty-five. Young men and women alike, in their teens and early twenties, are naturally more interested in their own lives and their own futures than in their obligations to their fellows; more inclined to emphasize what their elders owe to them than what they owe to their successors. The men continue in paid employment, but the majority of women leave it on marriage, when they are still young. It is not easy to convince the young woman worker that trade unionism matters, when she knows that she is likely to leave her job in a year or two; or to make her feel a responsibility for the young girl who will step into her job. The young married woman with children, who has been out of industry for some years, is often much more interested in the purpose and value of trade unionism than when she was in the factory. It is a tribute to the trade unions which organize women workers and especially to the qualities of their women officers that among the mass of youthful women workers there are many ardent trade unionists working for improved conditions in a firm or an industry which they expect soon to leave for good.

The fact that the majority do leave, as they believe, for good, is the chief handicap to their effective organization, to the raising of wage levels, and to an enlargement of their opportunities : this and the fact that when they leave it is to enter an occupation in which there is no payment—the management of a home and the care of a family.

This is the largest of all women's occupations. Among women over 14 at the last census, $7\frac{1}{2}$ millions were married women with no paid occupation ; and $5\frac{1}{2}$ million were gainfully employed, of whom fewer than 900,000 were married women.

The point is often made that the inferior status of women in industry and their comparatively weak organization reacts on the position of the homeworker. They affect her standard of living and that of her family, since the low wages of women tend to depress the general level of wages. But the point needs to be emphasized that the status of the woman in the home has its repercussions on the status and organization of the woman wage-earner. It is not only, or mainly, that the occupation of the great majority of adult women is one for which there is no wage payment ; it is rather the assumption that all the needs of the wife and mother in the home can be adequately voiced and met by her husband through his trade-union organization and in his capacity as breadwinner, which has tended to stifle trade-union initiative and independence on the part of the woman wage-earner. That assumption is being increasingly challenged by the woman in the home through her own organizations— Co-operative Guilds, Trade Union Guilds like the N.U.R.

Women's Guild, and the Women's Sections of the Labour Party. But so long as the view is accepted by the majority of men and women, including trade unionists, that the woman in the home should make no claim on the community except through another person, it is not surprising that many people who recognize the importance of the trade union for men think it of less importance for women; or that this attitude colours the outlook of the women workers who so badly need the protection that only a trade union can give. When the woman in the home makes demands in her own name through her own organizations, she is helping to raise the status of *all* women, both in industry and the home.

The work and status of the woman in the home, and what she herself is thinking about them, should have a big place in any discussion on the economic status of women. It is unfortunate that so many of those who claim to plead the cause of the married woman concentrate their attention on one fact—that her work is unpaid. Our outlook is so coloured by the cash values of a profit-making economic system, that we are apt to assume that to earn wages—a by-product in the business of earning profits for employers and share-holders—is the only basis of individual dignity and self-respect and independence. Certain feminists seem to argue that the married woman in the home is living in a state of perpetual economic sin, and that she must find salvation through wage-earning. The work she does in the home, they say, could be done very much better by other people. She should place her children in charge of experts, have her meals cooked by other experts at a communal restaurant, consign the washing to the expert care of a laundry, arrange for an expert domestic worker to come to her home with a vacuum cleaner and duster to do her cleaning, so that she herself may be raised to the dignity of a weekly pay packet. She will be a better mother to her children for the change (she will have some time for them at week-ends), and a better companion to her husband at the end of the day's work, than she used to be when she was a tired household drudge.

It is really an odd idea that the only work that is drudgery, the only work that can make a woman tired and cross is housework! But the whole picture is a middle-class composition. It ignores the quality of work and effort and organizing ability that go to the making of a home, especially a home where there are children. It ignores above all the hard fact that, for the average married woman, to have a job outside the home is to have two jobs—except in the case of a comparatively small number of women in highly-paid work. It is possible that we shall one day attain an economic order where this will no longer be true. No country, however, has solved the problem of how to protect the wife and mother who enters industrial employment from the strain and burden of two jobs. The married woman in industry has to combine so much housework with her wage-earning that she has too little time and energy for proper relaxation or to take her share in social or intellectual activities. This is contrary to all the theories of the feminists, but it happens to be the fact. In Lancashire, where it is customary for women to continue work in the cotton mills after marriage, because it takes the work of two people to earn a decent income, the women are loyal trade-union members, but though they are the majority of the union membership, they leave the business of the union to the men. Economic independence through wage-earning does not lift the working woman out of the " slavery " of the home.

Another school of thought, equally shocked by the wageless condition of the married woman, advocates wages for wives. There are two proposals : a payment by the State to the woman in the home as a recognition of her work ; and to confer on a wife the right to claim as wages a proportion of her husband's earnings. This again is thinking in terms which have no relation to working-class life and conditions. The difficulties and dangers of a State payment to a wife for her work are obvious. It opens possibilities of a degree of intrusion by the State inside the home which would not be tolerated in a democratic state, since, if the State pays for work, it would have a right to supervise its performance.

Those who sponsor the other suggestion of giving a woman a legal right to part of her husband's wages are apt to describe domestic life in terms which have little relation to common experience. From their fervent advocacy, it would seem that all married women are married unhappily, and to the same man—one who is a not very noble specimen of his sex. My own observation suggests that husbands are various ; that, as a class, they are as considerate and reasonable as any other class of human beings ; that quite a number of them, when they marry, become less selfish than their mothers did their best to make them. There are exceptions, husbands who conceal the amount of their earnings, who spend too much on their own personal pleasure, just as there are selfish wives.

The husband earns the wage, the wife controls its expenditure, the husband retaining a varying number of shillings for his own needs. That is the usual practice. The wife's job is often the more harassing of the two. It takes miracles of thought and planning to find the rent and feed and clothe the family. Most women who do that job have no patience with the suggestion that what is needed to ensure their economic independence is an Act of Parliament giving them a claim to five or ten or twenty shillings a week of their husband's pay. If the law said that to-morrow, it wouldn't make any difference to her work, to the amount of clothes she could buy for herself, to the number of times she could go to the cinema, or to what she could spare for the collection at the weekly meeting of her Guild or Women's Section. What would make a difference is an extra ten shillings in her husband's pay envelope, but she has a shrewd suspicion that the enthusiastic ladies who want to snatch her from degrading dependence on her husband are not interested in this idea!

The wife of a shipyard worker, writing me a year or two ago after attending a meeting on Wages for Wives said:

> If I insisted on a wage for myself out of my husband's wages my children would not be fed. . . . My husband and I have had an understanding about money matters since we married. We both do without lots of things for the sake of the children. We share together in occasional treats and small luxuries. It is the same with the married couples I know. To talk of wages for wives is nonsense under the present system. What is important in married life is a proper understanding about money, among other things. Without this there will be friction sometimes. But no Act of Parliament will save a wife from the consequences of her own foolishness in not coming to an understanding about money from the beginning.

That letter expresses what working-class housewives think. Marriage is not a commercial contract, but a partnership based on emotions which go to the roots of life. Both partners contribute in patience, understanding and goodwill to make it run smoothly. When money is tight, both go without for the sake of the children. When things are easier, the wife needs no Act of Parliament to give her a " right " to spend more on her own needs. Where the income is small she will see her husband properly fed even though she goes short herself. This is not an indication of wifely servitude but, in the circumstances, plain common sense, since he is the bread-winner for the family. Her humiliations are not due to her status as a wife, but to the economic conditions of her class.

If I have seemed so far negative it is because it is necessary that the attitude of the average working-class housewife to these middle-class nostrums should be stated. What is more important is what *she* thinks about her work, her status, and the changes she wants.

On the vexed question of the employment of married women there is only one attitude consistent with human dignity : every individual should have freedom of choice. Up to the war I think it is true to say that but for restrictions on the employment of married women, a considerable number of women would have continued paid work on marriage. On the other hand, the big majority of married women who were in industry were there from economic necessity. They had no choice. The bar imposed by many employers, including the Government and Local Authorities, on the employment of married women, is an indefensible invasion of freedom. Under the pressure of war needs the ban has been lifted in many directions—perhaps the only case where the war has led to an extension of individual liberty.

At the same time, with every restriction removed, there are some occupations where the married woman, and especially the young married woman, looking for a job, will be at a disadvantage because of the possibility that her employment will be interrupted by child-bearing. Since the war thousands of married women have gone into paid work, and as a result of this change, it is likely after the war that some of them will want to remain in industry. But there is no evidence of such an overwhelming change of outlook as to invalidate the view that the majority of women, if they were perfectly free to choose, would choose the home rather than industry. And I am pretty certain from views that have been expressed to me frequently and with vehemence in recent months that there will be a definite reaction against the employment of mothers of young children outside their homes.

While insisting on freedom of choice, I think it is socially undesirable that they should be so employed. Children are strange creatures—they need affection as well as vitamins, emotional security as well as physical security. Without emotional security, growth and development may be retarded or twisted. The source of that security is in the home, in the affection and care of the mother. There, too, is the source of many of the values which are the foundation of democracy. The mother who creates a happy home is rendering the nation valuable service : a compound of wisdom, common sense, affection and hard work. The work in itself is useful and important, though much of it is drudgery—unnecessary drudgery. But, judged by any rational scale of values, the unpaid work she does in the home is as valuable as a vast amount of outside work which women do for payment.

While the work done in the home cannot be paid as outside work is paid, housewives themselves are challenging the view that it deserves no recognition because it is unpaid. They insist that it should be judged by its social value. They recognize that those who are doing that job must depend on their own efforts, if its conditions are going to be improved and its status raised. They challenge the idea that they should rely on their husbands for the changes they want. The economic basis of the home depends on what the husband earns, so his trade union matters. But like miners and factory workers and shop workers who have made direct claims on the community for the improvement and protection of their working conditions, they too have claims to make for more tolerable conditions ; and, like the industrial workers they must be organized to make their demands effective.

One of the most significant changes since the last war has been the growth of the organizations which speak in the main for the woman in the home. They include the Women's Section of the Labour Party, of which I can speak with most knowledge. I am sometimes asked, " Why Women's Sections ? Men and women are equal politically, women are no longer inexperienced, why separate organization ? " If the Sections established in 1918 had only been a sort of kindergarten for politically inexperienced electors, until they were fit to enter the Local Party—the secondary school to which the men went direct—Sections would long ago have died a natural death. But they are and have always been much more than that. They are in fact a trade union for the woman in the home. Then membership is not confined to the married women, it is open to every woman member of the Party. In practice the Party members who enrol in the Sections and carry on their work are, in the main, the homekeeping women. The Sections have been a powerful and vital force in focussing attention on the problems of the home, and what housewives and mothers think about them. They have contributed also to an extent which cannot be measured to the Party both in organization and in policy. This can be illustrated from experience during the years of the most acute economic depression. Throughout the depressed areas, the women maintained their Sections even when the men were apathetic both about industrial and political organization. The contrast between the apathy of the men and the activity of the women was significant. It reflected the different angles from which the men and the women approached politics. The men view the world from workshop bench and pit shaft, the women from the home —both from the angle of their work. The men built their great organizations on their common experience in work. When the work was gone, men began to lose the sense of being needed in the community : in losing their work they lost the basis of their organization. But the wives of unemployed men kept their organizations going. The job in the home became more worrying and more difficult when the men lost their jobs—but the job was still there. The wives never knew, as their husbands knew, that terrible feeling of having no place in the community which prolonged unemployment brings. They still had a lively interest shared with their neighbours in their common work. So the Women's Sections continued vigorous and active. The women did something more than help to preserve a Party machine—they kept whole communities from succumbing to hopelessness and despair, to the sinister persuasiveness of totalitarian doctrines.

Through their Sections, Labour women not only foster a general interest in politics, they claim attention for their own special concerns. Theoretical demands for equality are not enough ; they want better conditions for women in those spheres where there can be no equality —in connection with child-bearing, child-care and the work of the home. They put forward these demands in their own right, not as the wives of their husbands. This may be illustrated by the changed attitude, e.g. on health services. Ten or fifteen years ago any national or local conference of Labour and Co-operative women would have adopted without a dissenting voice a resolution asking for the extension of medical treatment under the National Health Insurance Acts to wives and children. Such a resolution would have a slender chance of being carried to-day. Married women no longer ask to be tacked on to a service devised for their husbands and other workers outside the home. They are now demanding a national health service where the particular needs of women and children are properly provided for.

When last year, after persistent pressure on the Government, working-class housewives, through the Standing Joint Committee of Working Women's Organizations, compelled the Government in the Personal Injuries (Civilians) Scheme to recognize the housewife as a person entitled to compensation in her own right, and not as the wife of her husband, they started a revolution which will certainly encourage them to make further claims to be heard on all housewives' problems. No aspect of food policy has caused greater resentment among working-class women than the fact that while the Ministry of Food consults committees of producers and traders and trade unionists on food problems, there is no consultation with any representative committee of housewives whose work is more directly influenced by decisions on policy than any other section of workers.

The influence of organized women in public life since the last war is not seen in any particular change of opinion on general political issues, but rather in the admission to the agenda of politics of questions which are the direct concern of the wife and mother in the home. It may be argued that there are no women's questions, that every political question concerns both men and women. That in a sense is true. But there are miners' questions, there are textile questions. So too there are women's questions connected with the job that only women can do. The married women in the home see the way to an improvement of their status and a proper recognition of their work in insistence on the right to be heard on all these questions ; to formulate their own plans as to how the State should co-operate with them in their work, by the provision of better education and health services, and of labour-saving homes, cheapening labour-saving appliances, by control of the distribution and purity of food, by home-help schemes, and other services which will enable them to make the best of their job without the drudgery that wears out their health and strength to-day.

On the vexed question of children's allowances, the majority of organized women favour the principle, on certain conditions : only a State scheme providing for all children should be considered ; and any such scheme should not be regarded as a substitute for an extension of social services. Even if the burden of poverty which presses heavily on so many working-class homes were lifted, it would still be true that many of the needs of children can best be met collectively by the community rather than by the individual home.

I think that the experience of married women in industry during the war is likely to focus attention on certain more general questions of immense importance —for example, the effect of mechanization on the human being and especially on young workers. This is a question which the mothers of young factory workers have often discussed with me, with some bitterness, in recent years. Boys and girls are caught up by the machine at an age when their mental faculties need scope and freedom for growth. Work in a modern factory often stifles every creative faculty and leaves them with only enough energy in their leisure time to be passive consumers of mechanized entertainment. It is not only the question of conditions of factory work, but of the nature of much of the work. Is it possible to make good citizens for a democratic state out of young workers whose work gives them no creative satisfaction whatever? More leisure is part of the solution, but only part. How can we develop leisure-time activities that will be something more than an escape, that will provide compensation in a creative way for the sense of frustration and exhaustion caused by the nature and pace of work in the factory?

This is not a woman's question particularly. It is, however, a question which women, more than men, are likely to raise, for women naturally tend to keep in mind the human purposes for which politics and economic systems ought to exist. This perception of and emphasis on human issues come from their biological function and the work which that function assigns to them. It is sometimes counted against them as proof that they are not men's equals that they do not conform to the standards men have made in politics and public life. On the contrary, it is rather a proof that these standards are wrong. If we are to reach right conclusions and establish a properly balanced social organization, we need the qualities and the joint results of the experience of both men and women. A really civilized social system will give women not the right to be like men, but the right to be themselves (whatever that is—for until all *artificial* restrictions on women's freedom are gone we shall not know); will recognize that, whatever their differences, men and women are equal as human beings, and will, in its laws and institutions, give equal opportunity to and make equal use of the qualities, capacities, and experience of both.

## 5. CULTURE AND DEMOCRACY

### by GEORGE ORWELL

THE word Democracy is habitually used in two meanings which are quite different and are not even complementary to each other, but which are somehow felt to go together. One is the primary sense of the word—a form of society in which power is in the hands of the common people. The other is much vaguer but is more nearly what we mean when we speak of democracy in such a context as this. It means a form of society in which there is considerable respect for the individual, a reasonable amount of freedom of thought, speech and political organization, and what one might call a certain decency in the conduct of the government. It is this rather than any definite political system that we mean by democracy when we contrast it with totalitarianism.

Now in an essay of this sort I don't need to debunk the first definition. I don't need to point out that in England or in any western democracy power is not in fact in the hands of the common people. On the other hand, and particularly in left-wing circles, I think it *is* necessary to say that democracy in the other sense —freedom of speech, respect for the individual and all the rest of it—does have a reality, an importance, which cannot be made away with by mere juggling with words. Nothing is easier, particularly if you have a screen of battleships between you and danger, than to prove in words or on paper that there is no real difference between totalitarianism and " bourgeois " democracy. I haven't the slightest doubt that each of my readers has said that. I have said it frequently. It is the easiest thing in the world to show that all the compulsions which are put upon the individual crudely and openly in a totalitarian state are put upon him in a slightly more subtle way by the money-squeeze in a so-called democratic society. After all, if the Germans are very cruel to the Poles, our own behaviour is not so very nice in India. There are concentration camps in Germany, but didn't we ourselves pen up a lot of innocent people behind barbed wire last year? The S.S. and the Gestapo are horrible things, but if you lived in the slums of Liverpool you probably wouldn't think of the police as angels. Freedom of thought isn't technically restricted in England, but in practice the whole of the Press that matters is in the hands of a small clique of millionaires who can prevent you from saying what you think. Everybody knows that line of thought. It is impossible to go into a left-wing gathering anywhere without hearing it put forward. But I think it is necessary to recognize that it is not only nonsense, but nonsense of a kind which can only be uttered by people who have a screen of money and ships between themselves and reality. For when one has pointed out the essential unfreedom of democratic society, and its similarity with totalitarian society, there does remain the residual difference that in a country like this we are not afraid to stand up and say what we think. Quite probably there is a secret police in England, but the point is that we don't feel afraid of it. I may often have had detectives listening to speeches I have made, but I could safely ignore their presence. The fact is that all demonstrations that totalitarianism and democracy are the same thing—democracy and fascism are twins, in Stalin's words—boil down to saying that a difference of degree is not a difference. This is a fallacy which is as old as history. There is even a Greek name for it which I have forgotten. It is perhaps not particularly important that I can write what I like for a limited public whose influence will extend to a few hundreds more, but it *is* important, symptomatically important at any rate, that after two years of war, during most of which we have been in a very serious jam, I don't feel *more* frightened of doing so than I did two years ago. Even if it could be shown to be true that there is no real difference between democracy and totalitarianism, what at least is never true is that people *feel* them to be the same.

I think what this demonstrates is that not only is there a real difference between old forms of society like our own, which have had the chance to develop a certain decency in their politics, and the newer totalitarian states, but that our type of society is incapable of changing in certain directions unless forcibly altered from the outside. There are certain values which it seems not to lose touch with, even in moments of deadly danger. But notice that I say only that our form of democracy can't of its own accord change in certain directions, not that it can't change at all. It is certain that it *must* change or perish. If there is one thing in the world that is certain, it is that capitalistic democracy in its present form cannot survive. Imagine for a moment that we are not at war and are back in Chamberlain's dear dead days; in those circumstances, if I had to establish that capitalist democracy cannot survive, I think I should do it by pointing out that what are now called democratic nations are not reproducing themselves. Most of the breeding of the world is done in non-democratic countries. As soon as the standard of living rises beyond a certain point and people have a certain power of doing what they want, the birth-rate always falls below replacement level. And that is not due to economic insecurity, which is the fashionable explanation. It is sheer nonsense to say that there is less economic security in Britain and the

United States than in the great breeding centres of China and India.  On the contrary, it is due to something that goes with capitalist democracy, and that is the principle of hedonism.  Our birth-rate is small because people are taught to have a consumer mentality.  The chief feature of life in capitalist society during the past twenty years has been an endless struggle to sell goods which there is never enough money to buy ; and this has involved teaching ordinary people that things like cars, refrigerators, movies, cigarettes, fur coats and silk stockings are more important than children.  However, there is a more immediate argument against the survival of capitalist democracy arising from the fact that we are at war.  Once again I don't have to insult left-wing circles by pointing out the weaknesses of a capitalist nation at war.  If I were lecturing to readers of the *Daily Telegraph* I should point out that in capitalist society the making of profits is and must be one's main motive, and I should point for example to such things as the fact that in the last week before the outbreak of war people in England were tumbling over one another in their eagerness to sell lead, nickel, copper, rubber, shellac, and so forth, to Germany, in the full knowledge that these things would come back on them in the form of bombs in a few months' time.  But when I am writing for a predominantly socialist public, I hardly need to point out the structural weaknesses of capitalist democracy which will force it to change or perish.  I prefer to insist on certain weaknesses which are inflicted on us by the hedonistic principle, and by the fact that in a democracy people are called on to vote upon things which in practice they know nothing about.

One of the worst things about democratic society in the last twenty years has been the difficulty of any straight talking or thinking.  Let me take one important fact,

I might say *the* basic fact about our social structure. That is, that it is founded on cheap coloured labour. As the world is now constituted, we are all standing on the backs of half-starved Asiatic coolies. The standard of living of the British working class has been and is artificially high because it is based on a parasitic economy. The working class is as much involved in the exploitation of coloured labour as anybody else, but so far as I know, nowhere in the British Press in the last twenty years—at any rate in no part of the Press likely to get wide attention —do you find any clear admission of that fact or any straight talking about it. In the last twenty years there were really two policies open to us as a nation living on coloured labour. One was to say frankly : We are the master-race—and remember, that is how Hitler talks to his people, because he is a totalitarian leader and can speak frankly on certain subjects—we are the master-race, we live by exploiting inferior races, let's all get together and squeeze as much out of them as we can. That was one policy ; that was what, shall we say, *The Times* ought to have said if it had had the guts. It didn't say it. The other possible policy was to say something like this : We cannot go on exploiting the world for ever, we must do justice to the Indians, the Chinese and all the rest of them, and since our standard of living is artificially high and the process of adjustment is bound to be painful and difficult, we must be ready to lower that standard of living for the time being. Also, since powerful influences will be at work to prevent the underdog from getting his rights, we must arm ourselves against the coming international civil war, instead of simply agitating for higher wages and shorter hours. That is what, for instance, the *Daily Herald* would have said if it had had the guts. Once again, nowhere will you find anything like that in plain words. You simply couldn't say that kind of thing in newspapers which had to live off their circulation and off advertisements for consumption goods. One result of this lack of straight talking was complete inability to prepare for the present war. I don't point to the part played by the Right. That is obvious. But the part played by the Left, which was due to the inherent contradiction in a political party which actually existed to defend wages but which liked to think of itself as having internationalist aims, was almost equally damaging to ourselves. In effect, the policy of the English Left has always been Disarmament and War. It has always stood for a vigorous foreign policy without being willing or able to point out to ordinary people that very heavy sacrifices are necessary in order to pay for the armaments without which a vigorous foreign policy is impossible.

For purposes of demonstration, I have picked out just one fact basic to our situation about which it has been impossible, in the sort of society we have been living in, to tell the truth. No politician in the last twenty years who told the truth about the British Empire could have got himself a political following. And I think one can see from this the inevitable weakness of any democratic society when challenged by other societies which are not democratic, which are ruled by clear-sighted, evil men who know exactly what they want, who don't have to consider things like trade unions or newspapers dependent on advertisements for consumption goods, and who have no difficulty in forcing whole populations to work like slaves and breed like rabbits. In addition, another less noticeable but in the long run equally important factor is the peculiar character of the intelligentsia that grows up in a wealthy capitalist democracy. Our intelligentsia, I mean the left-wing intelligentsia—and please notice that in the last ten years there has been no intelligentsia in England that is not more or less " Left "—is essentially the product of investment capital. It owes its peculiarities partly to that and partly to the exceptional security of our life in England. The thing that always strikes one about the British intelligentsia is its extraordinarily negative outlook, its lack of any firm beliefs or positive aims, and its power of harbouring illusions that would not be possible to people in less sheltered places. In an essay of this length I cannot give an exhaustive list of the illusions of the British intelligentsia. As an example I will take just one obviously silly, obviously fallacious idea which is almost peculiar to Anglo-Saxon civilization, namely Pacifism. Pacifism as put forward by, for instance, the Peace Pledge Union, is such nonsense that no one who has ever been forced into contact with realities would even consider it. Anyone who has any notion at all of the way in which things happen knows that a government which will not use force can always be overthrown by any body of people, even by any one individual, that is less scrupulous. Society as we know it *must* in the last instance be founded on force. A child of six would be able to see that. But in England we have lived for decades past in this extraordinary sheltered state in which you can go your whole life without, for instance, ever seeing a dead man, without ever receiving a blow, without ever spending a night in the open or feeling hungry—without, in consequence, ever needing to look down at the roots on which your own existence is founded. In that kind of atmosphere extraordinary follies are possible and can infect all sorts of people. One can see the result in the attitude of the British intelligentsia towards the present war, which began, in my opinion, about 1935 or 1936, definitely not later than 1936. Between 1935 and 1939 the whole of the left-wing intelligentsia, almost like a flock of sheep, were pro-war. They were in favour of making a firm stand against Germany, although on the whole they were also against arming. Immediately war broke out the left-wing intelligentsia turned anti-war. This was not due to the Russo-German Pact and to the feeling that one must justify Russian policy at all costs. It affected a lot of people who were not particularly pro-Russian in sentiment, and to my knowledge others who were pro-Russian in sentiment did not change their anti-war views on June 22nd. I suggest that this was simply due to the unrealistic attitude which it has been possible to develop in the last twenty years and the mere tendency to discontent which any thinking person has in our kind of society. The best place in which to study the English left-wing mind is the weekly paper, the *New Statesman*, which is a sort of crossing ground for the various intellectual currents of the Left. As a magazine the *New Statesman* seems to me to have only symptomatic value. I have been a regular reader of it for many years and never once have I found in it any coherent policy or any constructive suggestion—anything, in fact, except a general gloom and an automatic discontent with whatever happens to be in progress at the moment. It expresses nothing except the fact that English left-wing intellectuals of all shades do not like the society they are living in but at the same time do not want to face the effort or the responsibility of changing it.

Now notice that all I have said hitherto could have been printed in one of those snooty little minor leading articles in *The Times*. It sounds just like the conventional attack on " highbrows " which A. P. Herbert, etc., are so fond of. But it is very important to realize that there is another side to the question. Why is it that a wealthy capitalist society seems naturally to breed a discontented intelligentsia like a sort of wart on its surface? The reason is that in such a society as ours the intelligentsia is functionless. In the last twenty years, particularly in Britain and America and almost as much in France, there has been no real job, no place in the structure of society, for the thinking man as such. If he has had a job at all it is only owing to the fact that there is a lot of invested capital knocking about, hence a lot of interest, which goes into the pockets of decadent third-generation rentiers, who spend it in financing picture galleries and literary reviews, which in turn provide an income for artists genuine and spurious. There has been no opportunity for the thinking man, as such, to make himself or feel himself *useful*. This condition persists even when the nation is at war, and even in the most desperate moments of war. I remember early in the war I was talking to the editor of a left-wing weekly paper, and he said to me, " You know Sir Stafford Cripps wrote to the Government on the first day of the war offering his services in any capacity." I said, " So did I." My friend, let's call him X, said, " So did I, but the difference is that Cripps was distinguished enough to get an answer "—the answer being negative, of course. There you have a picture of the humiliating position of the intelligentsia in our type of society. If the Government can use them at all, it uses them not for the talents they actually possess but at best can only turn them into rather inefficient private soldiers or unreliable clerks. And if that is the case in war it is even more so in peace. Look at a map of the world and you will see that nearly a quarter of it is painted red. That is the British Empire—and remember that in spite of all things it is on the whole better to be inside the British Empire than outside it. Well, the whole of that vast empire is administered by people who cannot be called in the narrow sense intellectuals, people who have no contact with the intelligentsia whatever.

The intelligentsia during the last twenty years could not take part in that process of administration because the Empire and all its workings were so out of date, so manifestly unjust, that they would necessarily have revolted against it. They lived in a society which automatically deprived them of function and in which the best way to prosper was to be stupid. That is the explanation of their never-failing discontent. In every other way they had opportunities such as the world has never before seen. They had ease, money, security, liberty of thought and even completer moral liberty. Life in Bloomsbury during the last twenty years has been what the moral rebels all through the ages have dreamed about. And yet on the whole the people who were favoured in this way weren't happy, didn't really like the things they ostensibly asked for. They would sooner have had a genuine function in a society which might give them less but took them more seriously.

I have outlined shortly, as examples, just one or two of the inherent weaknesses of capitalist democracy. If you draw a caricature of capitalist democracy you get a picture something like this : at the top a wealthy class living largely on dividends ; living on them an enormous army of professional men, servants, tradesmen, psychoanalysts, interior decorators and whatnot ; also living on them is a parasitic intelligentsia, earning their keep by pretending to abuse the people who pay them—having the same sort of function in fact as a dog's fleas, which the dog mildly enjoys snapping at ; and at the bottom you get a working class with artificially high standards and permanently on strike for the means to buy refrigerators, electric cookers, lipsticks and radiograms. That is an untrue picture, but remember that it is only untrue in the way in which a caricature is untrue. That is how a wealthy country like England appears from the outside.

That is how the Italian radio propagandists, for instance, describe us, and though of course they are lying and exaggerating, they do believe a part of what they say.

I claim that a society with these weaknesses, particularly when it is in a desperate predicament, must change or perish. All that I have said of Britain is *a fortiori* true of the U.S.A. I never pick up an American magazine or go to an American film without feeling that if these things are really representative of the American scene, a society of that kind will not stand the shock of war without fundamental change. If our society survives it must survive in a more disciplined, hardened form, with its fat sweated off it and the profit motive abolished. But in saying that, haven't I come near to giving the game away and saying that in order to fight successfully against our enemies we must become exactly like them? The pacifists have a formula, which is easy to repeat and needs no thought, "If you fight against fascism you go fascist yourself." That is a mechanistic form of thought. When a pacifist says to me, "If you fight fascism you become fascist yourself," I always answer, "And if you fight against negroes you turn black." The fact that they usually take several minutes to see the fallacy gives you an idea of the quality of their minds. Actually, to say that by fighting against Nazi Germany we must become exactly like Nazi Germany is to lack any historical sense whatever. The reason why Germany took a particular line of development is contained in the history of Germany, and the reason why England is taking a different line is contained in the history of England. It is important to realize that we *are* taking a different line. Certain things which ought to have happened if the mechanical formula which I mentioned just now were correct, have not happened and show no signs of happening. I come back to the fact that I am

not frightened to take my pen and write in this vein—
that I am not frightened, if I choose, to say that this
is an imperialist war and Churchill is the tool of
the capitalist class and that we ought to stop fighting
to-morrow. As I said earlier, and it can hardly be
repeated too often, the significant thing is not that I can
say this, but that I am not *more* frightened of saying it
after two years of desperate war in which it is certainly
not to the advantage of the Government to have people
walking about and saying things of this kind. What
that implies is the failure of our society, perhaps its actual
lack of power, to develop in a certain direction. There
is no sign of any authentically fascist development in
Britain at this time. Certain things which could lead
to fascism are inevitably going on. Inevitably a centralization of power is taking place, and equally inevitably
there is conscription of labour, but the failure beyond
a certain point to tamper with freedom of speech indicates
that there is no real growth of fascist mentality. The
average left-wing intellectual will tell you in his mechanistic way that Churchill is a fascist. Here he is using
words in the same manner as Goebbels when he says that
Chiang Kai Shek is a Jew. The truth is that the British
ruling class are too old-fashioned to develop in a genuinely
fascist direction. Let me take one small fact which is
symptomatically important—the prohibition in all totalitarian countries of listening in to foreign broadcasts. It
is known that the B.B.C. is listened in to all over Europe
with passion, though when people are allowed to listen
in to the B.B.C. the tendency is rather the opposite. As
long as that prohibition exists, the inference must inevitably be drawn that that broadcast which you are forbidden
to listen to is probably true. The Germans have an
excellent series of broadcasts to England, including a
number of spurious stations pretending to be " Freedom "

stations inside the British Isles, but nobody listens to them, because it is not forbidden. Now the people directing German propaganda are not fools. You can see from Goebbels's speeches that he is aware that if he could only lift the ban people would stop listening to the B.B.C., but he cannot do so because the notion of giving a free hearing to an enemy is contradictory to the whole fascist outlook. Our own Government is a much more old-fashioned despotism, the kind of pre-fascist despotism which does not care what you think so long as your outward actions are correct. The totalitarian mentality hardly exists here as yet. Hardly anybody lies awake quivering with rage and hatred because somebody a little further down the street is committing " deviations ". And I suggest that this failure to develop a totalitarian mental atmosphere, even when the material conditions for it exist, is a sign that provided we can avoid conquest from without, our society will not lose touch with certain habits and values which have been its mark for hundreds of years.

In all this talk about Democracy I have strayed a long way from the other word in the title of this chapter—Culture. As before, the word has at least two meanings. People speak of " culture " in an anthropological sense and in an aesthetic sense. You discover, for instance, an island somewhere in the South Seas where the people practice cannibalism and worship the sun ; that is " a culture ". Or you buy a copy of the *Oxford Book of English Verse* and learn quotable bits by heart ; that is " Culture ". But you find a certain connection between the two meanings if you go back to the primary sense of the word. Culture means controlled growth. Any bit of soil will grow plants if it gets enough water, but so long as they grow higgledy-piggledy we call that " Nature ". As soon as it is ploughed and things are planted in rows

we say that it is " cultivated ". But we also speak of
soil reaching a high state of culture. If you merely
plough up a piece of virgin soil you cannot grow particularly fine products on it ; you could not produce the
best French wines, or even good peas or asparagus, from
a soil of that type. If you till a piece of soil long enough
and deep enough, and enrich it in the right way, you can
change its whole nature and texture, even its colour.
You only do that in order to grow finer plants on it, so
that ultimately the value of a soil is judged by its products. So in the long run is a civilization. We say that
a civilization has reached a high state of culture when
each generation leaves behind a residue of certain things
which one can describe roughly as art and wisdom.
Almost inevitably a civilization is judged by the art it
leaves behind. It is perhaps possible to imagine a high
civilization existing as it were in a vacuum, each generation getting a tremendous kick out of life but leaving
nothing behind, but, in the nature of things, we have
no evidence of any such thing having ever existed. On
the other hand, when you dig up some ruined city in the
Central American forests and find remarkable sculptures,
you say, simply on the evidence of the sculptures, " This
was a high civilization, these people had reached a high
state of culture." Art is an important symptom. It is
a registration, as it were, of man's attitude to the universe
at any given moment. A good civilization will produce
good works of art, not as its main purpose but as its most
important by-product. And in a civilization which is
really sound this will apply not only to what we call fine
art, but to all the domestic and applied arts—furniture,
clothes, houses, pottery, glass, tools and whatnot. They
are all, even down to such things as the designs on stamps
and coins, symptomatic of the prevailing culture.

Now, when I extend what I am saying to cover such

things as clothes and furniture, I may seem to be giving up the cause of culture as lost. For though our age may have produced good major art—I only say " may ", you notice—it is unquestionable that in all the minor arts it is an age of unbearable ugliness. You can see more ugly things in Oxford Street in half an hour than you could see among all the savage tribes in the world. What has happened to us, of course, and temporarily thrown our culture off the rails, is the impact of the machine. I am not one of those people who talk as though we could suddenly cut ourselves loose from the machine civilization and return to the Middle Ages. Whatever else history may do, it never travels backwards. But there is no use blinking the fact that when you move into the industrial era you have to pass through an age, perhaps centuries long, of the most horrible ugliness. A primitive person compared with ourselves appears at first sight to have perfect taste. His clothes, for instance, are never ugly. Even if he is dressed only in a bit of cloth no bigger than a handkerchief, he will wear it gracefully. There is a queer little confession of the aesthetic inferiority of Western man in a rule which exists or existed till recently in the British army. A British private soldier is rarely allowed to wear civilian clothes. On the other hand, in the Indian army the sepoys when off duty are always allowed to wear their own clothes, because it is known that, being Indians, they can be trusted to dress themselves becomingly. An Englishman cannot, unless he has had a special kind of training, and even then he is only what is called " well dressed " according to what is no more than an accepted code of ugliness. And yet when one looks deeper one sees that this seeming superiority of taste in the primitive or savage man is an illusion. For the good taste of the primitive collapses with extraordinary promptitude as soon as he comes into contact with machine civilization. Not only does he eagerly seize the most vulgar products of the machine—offer him a five-shilling enamelled German wrist-watch and he grabs it with both hands—but his whole aesthetic sense seems to disappear at the first contact. I have seen an Indian dressed only in a loin-cloth and a bowler hat. Even we would not do a thing like that. But so long as he sticks to his original form of dress he has, apparently, perfect taste. The explanation is that throughout long ages he has lived in a culture in which there has been very little change. A certain way of life has been built up, and even the minutest details, even such things as gestures and movements of the body, have been gradually perfected, so that there is not much chance for any one individual to go wrong. We, on the other hand, happen to live at a moment when there is every opportunity to go wrong. We have moved suddenly into the period of machine civilization, which is the most drastic change that has happened in thousands of years. But I think that the idea of a complete and final loss of culture is an illusion. For we made once before an equally drastic change, when we changed from a nomadic to an agricultural way of life, and after all, a new culture was built up. At present we are merely in the process of development, and given a certain continuity one can even prophesy to some small extent what our culture will be like when we possess one again. To say that the present age is cultureless is rather like saying that I am beardless. I have never let my beard grow, but it is potentially there, and up to a point I can tell you what it would be like if it existed. I can tell you that it wouldn't be red, for instance. So also with culture. I can't tell you what our civilization will be like in A.D. 2200, but I think I could prophesy some of its characteristics. I think I can foretell, for instance, that we shall still be using the English language and that it will still have something in common with the English of Shakespeare, always assuming that we have escaped conquest from without.

At the moment that is the crucial point. We are temporarily in the position of having to fight rearguard actions in defence of what is left of civilization, but I don't think there is any reason to be pessimistic about the long-term effects of the arrival of the machine. Ultimately we shall get used to the machine. We do, however, have to defend ourselves against the threat of totalitarianism, which might really bring a swift and final death to civilization. Why is it that everything we mean by culture is menaced by totalitarianism? Because totalitarianism menaces the existence of the individual, and the last four or five hundred years have put the individual so emphatically on the map that it is hard for us to imagine him off it again. To illustrate the impact of totalitarianism on culture I will name only a single art, literature, which in the form in which we know it is incompatible with the totalitarian form of government. At first sight it may seem like begging the question to choose literature rather than any other art, because literature is the one in which the line between fine art and propaganda is hardest to draw, and consequently is the one most immediately affected by political changes. But if the implications are followed up it will be found that in every art, even including such things as pottery or cabinet-making, the interference with the emotions of the individual peculiar to totalitarianism are equally deadening. Why is it that individual literature is incompatible with totalitarianism? We are in the habit of saying that the Nazis are the enemies of literature, but they would prefer not to be its enemies if they knew how to avoid it. If they could suddenly produce a Shakespeare and say, " This is *our* Shakespeare," they would be only too delighted. The reason is that the driving force, the dynamo as you might say, of any artist is his emotions, and his emotions do not necessarily correspond to the political necessity of the moment. The totalitarian state exists for the glorification of the ruling clique, which means that the ruling clique are the prisoners of their own power and are obliged to follow any policy, no matter how self-contradictory, which will keep them in power. And having followed their policy they are obliged to justify it, so that all thought becomes a rationalization of the shifts of power politics. It is not true that an atmosphere of orthodoxy is in itself fatal to literature. To realize that you have only got to think for a moment of the Middle Ages. In the Middle Ages men lived within a framework of thought which was as rigid, I suppose, as the one in which people have to live in Germany to-day. And yet not only could they produce good literature—and in the later Middle Ages it was distinctly *individual* literature—but the thing that always strikes me about the few medieval writers I know is the comparative freedom of their minds. Catholic belief was more or less obligatory, but it didn't cripple them. The difference, of course, is that in the Middle Ages the prevailing orthodoxy *didn't change*, or at least didn't change suddenly. It probably doesn't matter that men should be compelled to live within a certain framework of thought. Everyone's mind is necessarily full of beliefs which he has accepted from the outside and entirely on trust. I couldn't prove, for instance, that the world is round. I could give good reasons for thinking that it is not flat, but to prove that it is round needs pages of mathematics which I should be incapable of understanding. But this unproven belief is something which I have grown up with and never questioned, and which consequently doesn't cause any emotional disturbance in me. On the other hand, if someone suddenly comes to me with a loaded pistol and tells me that I have got to believe that Jews are not human beings, it does something to my emotional life which would necessarily have a damaging effect on any creative work I attempted.

You see there a striking difference between capitalist democracy as it now exists, and totalitarianism. In England, absurdities just as great as any in the totalitarian states are being offered to you all the time, but you are not under any obligation to accept them. Six months ago, for example, Stalin was Bad with a big B. Now he is Good with a big G. A year ago the Finns were Good. Now they are Bad. Mussolini is Bad at this moment, but it would not particularly surprise me to see him Good within a year. But after all, nobody is compelled to swallow this kind of thing. If I write a book I am not forced to say in it that Stalin is Good, I don't have to watch with desperate anxiety lest there should be a political change before the book goes to press, my emotional life is not interfered with. In a totalitarian state it is difficult to imagine any writing above the level of pamphleteering. Here somebody may answer, " But in fact some of the best writers of our time have come to terms with Fascism." This is one of those statements which tend to dissolve when you examine them. It is perfectly true that up to about 1930 the best European writers were on the whole reactionary in tendency, but if they were inclined for a while to be pro-Fascist it was because they made the mistake, which was easy to make before Hitler was in power, of thinking that Fascism was a form of Conservatism. Since then the issue has become clearer, but even so it is possible to make out an impressive list of writers who have accepted Fascism outright. Céline, author of *Voyage au Bout de la Nuit*, is now Exhibit

A in Paris, or at least his books are. Ezra Pound is in Rome doing anti-Semitic broadcasts. Wyndham Lewis for a long time had connections with Mosley's movement, and so had Osbert Sitwell. Roy Campbell fought for Franco in Spain. And there is a long list of French writers who have gone over to the Nazis since the fall of France. All this, however, is somewhat misleading. Roy Campbell and Wyndham Lewis have certainly changed some of their opinions during the last few years, and we don't know much as yet about the motives of the various French writers who have capitulated. Of the writers I mentioned just now, the one whom it is most possible to respect is Céline. There is no question about the venomously anti-left and anti-Jewish tendency of the stuff he has written during the past ten years. But I don't think he can be taken as proof that it is possible for good writers, intelligent, scrupulous men, to make their peace with Fascism. He is simply a good mind gone sour. His writings are essentially an expression of disgust with modern life. I think I described him once as a voice from the cesspool. Rather as Eliot, Maritain and others reacted against the idealistic League of Nations atmosphere of the nineteen-twenties, Céline reacted against the half-baked left-wing orthodoxy of the following decade, and because he was a man in whom disgust and hatred were the chief driving force, he went the whole way, anti-semitism and all. He accepted Nazism as a kind of nihilism. From the Nazi point of view Céline would obviously come under the heading of kulturbolschewsmus, but as he happens to bear a distinguished name, the Nazis are quite unscrupulous enough to use him against intellectuals elsewhere, as an example of a literary man who has seen the light. But obviously this is no more than a first-generation phenomenon. You can't imagine a literary tradition founded on *Voyage au Bout de la Nuit* and *Mea Culpa*. You can't imagine generation after generation of Célines, all founding their work upon disgust and horror of contemporary life—and certainly that is not the kind of literary tradition that the Nazis want to establish. Céline, or any writer like him, is simply a disgruntled individual who can be temporarily made use of in a moment of chaos.

I think one must conclude that literature as we know it is inseparable from the sanctity of the individual, and therefore is absolutely incompatible with the totalitarian way of life. And what is true of literature is true of nearly everything that we classify under the heading of culture. One must conclude therefore that though our democracy is bound to change—can, in fact, only survive by turning into Socialism—all that we mean by culture is inextricably bound up with democratic values. The destruction of democracy would mean not simply the loss of certain advantages and the acquisition of certain others, but an actual *end* to civilization as we know it. We must defend ourselves against that as we should defend ourselves against an invasion from Mars, because we can hardly imagine an alternative.

But let nothing that I have said be taken as meaning that at this moment we have much in the way of a culture to defend. We are only fighting for the future. We are in the trough of the wave, though we know that presently the wave will go up again. We are not the flowers of a civilization, we only know that, given growth, given continuity, at some time civilization will flower again. In this age we can at best be only the manure of the future. On that perhaps rather depressing note I will conclude.

For Product Safety Concerns and Information please contact our EU
representative GPSR@taylorandfrancis.com
Taylor & Francis Verlag GmbH, Kaufingerstraße 24, 80331 München, Germany

www.ingramcontent.com/pod-product-compliance
Lightning Source LLC
Chambersburg PA
CBHW070543300426
44113CB00011B/1775